100
RUNS
OF A LIFETIME

100
RUNS
OF A LIFETIME

The World's Ultimate Races and Trails

BART YASSO

NATIONAL GEOGRAPHIC

WASHINGTON, D.C.

CONTENTS

LEFT: Kenyan long-distance runner Eliud Kipchoge (center left) waits with other eager athletes at the starting line of the 2023 Boston Marathon.

PAGES 2-3: Switzerland's Valais region contains more than 5,000 miles (8,040 km) of trails through mountains, meadows, and forests.

PAGES 6-7: The Rio de Janeiro Marathon takes runners past the city's renowned Atlantic beaches.

INTRODUCTION

I n 1995, I was standing at the bottom of Ngorongoro Crater in Tanzania. I had taken a guided jeep tour to the bottom of the largest intact caldera in the world, a place inhabited by some of the most majestic creatures I'd ever seen—lions, leopards, rhinoceroses, elephants, and more. The area is home to 115 different protected species, and this experience was a dream realized (I've always been a devout animal lover, drawn to African safaris). But standing at the bottom of the crater, I couldn't shake the feeling of wanting to run the 2,000 feet (610 m) up the dirt road to our camp on the rim. It seemed like such a special place to add to the many locations I'd logged miles since I started running in 1977.

Our tour guide was dubious, however. He didn't know if the wildlife would take kindly to a human charging up the trail. But I promised to stick close to the 4×4 and jump in if we had any dangerous encounters. He relented and we started our adventure up the crater wall, my choppy gait gradually ascending the rutted, rough terrain. By the time we crested the top, I had spotted only a lone hyena, and it was uninterested in the man closely following a slow-moving jeep. We kept going, making it to our home base just in time to catch a quintessential sunset. The blazing oranges, yellows, and pinks lit up the uninterrupted western horizon before us.

In that moment, I knew I had just completed my run of a lifetime. A run in a place that felt sacred to me.

I discovered running as a 21-year-old looking for direction and, perhaps, some discipline. A local 10K near my eastern Pennsylvania home changed my life completely. The feeling of accomplishment that I found in the sport gave me much needed purpose. I quickly learned that the work I put into running didn't just translate into better performances and results (it did, of course), but it also connected me more deeply to a global community of people who shared my passion for movement and good health. It eventually led me to

COMMON RACE DISTANCE CONVERSIONS

1 mile = 1.6 kilometers

5K = 3.1 miles

10K = 6.2 miles

12K = 7.4 miles

15K = 9.3 miles

10 miles = 16.1 kilometers

Half-marathon = 13.1 miles/ 21.1 kilometers

Marathon = 26.2 miles/ 42.2 kilometers

ABOVE: **The author, wearing bib number 35, crosses the Bixby Bridge, the half-way point of the Big Sur International Marathon.**

PAGES 10-11: **A runner finds the strength for a celebratory kick to end the 155-mile (250 km) 2024 Marathon des Sables in Ouarzazate, Morocco.**

PAGES 12-13: **South Africa's Table Mountain offers multiple trail options.**

Runner's World magazine, where I served as the chief running officer for 30 years. As the ambassador of the publication, I traveled to races and events all over the world, spreading the gospel of running—mostly the joy and camaraderie it creates. Eventually, I became known as the unofficial "Mayor of Running," and spent my entire adult life encouraging others to participate, at whatever level or intensity they wanted. This work became my calling.

Through my extensive range of experiences, I've learned that a "run of a lifetime" can happen anywhere, at any time—maybe impulsively at the bottom of a volcanic crater or, less whimsically, at a big race that was the culmination of a detailed training plan. A run of a lifetime means something different to everybody. It can be completing your very first mile down a neighborhood bike path, clocking your fastest 5K, or finishing the Antarctica Marathon (page 258).

The truth is, the places we put one foot in front of the other often take us to corners of the earth we'd otherwise never see or notice. Sometimes all we need is a suggestion, a little inspiration, or a reason to explore somewhere new. That's why I've compiled 100 different routes and races that have brought meaning and memories to my life in this collection—and I hope they do the same for you. Whether you're looking for shorter distances, a marathon event, an ultra race, or just a far-flung trail to traverse, this book features my all-time favorites, giving you a taste of what you'll experience out on the course, ideas for postrace meals and prerace shakeout runs (a two- to three-mile [3.2–4.8 km] easy run the day before your event), and inside tips for making the most of your running travels.

It's a privilege to share my collection of lifetime adventures. Running around the world has revealed fortitude and strength I never knew I had. It has brought long-lasting friendships with people I would have never met otherwise. Fast or slow, flat or steep, trail or road—wherever your run takes you, I hope you find the same kind of delight and wonder that every starting line has brought me. Here's to your next adventure, and mine too.

PART ONE

SHORT-DISTANCE & ROAD RACES

The Monument Avenue 10K takes runners past historic homes in Richmond, Virginia (page 66).

GARDEN OF THE GODS

Your choice of race in an epic setting of sandstone monoliths and rolling hills

SEASON: Summer   **TOTAL NO. OF RUNNERS:** 2,000   **RACE DISTANCES:** 10K; 10K trail; 10 miles
SURFACE: Paved roads and sandstone trails   **DIFFICULTY:** Moderate

remember the first time I laid my eyes on a photo of the Garden of the Gods 10-miler. Back in 1980, *Runner's World* published a beautiful array of images showing runners amid the national natural landmark's astonishing sedimentary-rock spires, which explode from the earth's surface like Stone Age cathedrals. I knew right away this was a must-do race.

Garden of the Gods, a 1,300-acre (530 ha) park just five miles (8 km) from downtown Colorado Springs, rests on the eastern front of 14,115-foot (4,302 m) Pikes Peak, which provides a classic alpine backdrop and helps make the park a popular hiking, rock-climbing, and horseback-riding destination. Running conditions in this alpine desert reliably complement the terrific scenery. In early June, when the 10-miler is held, temperatures are typically in the low 60s Fahrenheit (15–20°C). You'll need sunscreen on race day (Colorado gets 300 days of sun every year, and you're at higher altitude), but you won't have to worry about layering.

Established in 1977, the race has three courses: the traditional 10-miler, as well as a 10K race and a 10K trail run. All three traverse rolling hills with a few steep climbs and descents—and all start and end at an elevation of 6,300 feet (1,920 m). The 10-miler has around 1,000 feet (300 m) of elevation gain, with the highest elevation on the course at around 6,500 feet (1,980 m).

Though the 10-miler and the 10K courses mostly follow paved roads, the

WHERE TO STAY

Colorado Springs is the place to stay for historic hotels and a great restaurant scene. The five-star Broadmoor resort opened in 1918 and looks like it was carved directly into the Rocky Mountains. You can rent a room or a cottage, and several restaurants are on premises. Alternatively, the four-star Antlers hotel is located right downtown and within walking distance of a dozen restaurants.

Runners take on the Juniper Way Loop at the 39th annual Garden of the Gods.

10K trail race meanders down many of the park's 21 miles (34 km) of beautiful dirt and crushed-sandstone routes. None of these paths is particularly technical. In fact, most are as free of rocks and debris as your typical suburban rail trail.

Whichever course you choose, you'll pass by towering sandstone formations, some 300 feet (90 m) high, including the famous Kissing Camels, Sleeping Giant, and (my personal favorite) Balanced Rock, which appears to defy gravity but has stood steadfastly in place for eons. The shared finish line for all three races is located at the historic Rock Ledge Ranch, a living history museum and farm right in the middle of the park. This is one of the coolest finishing areas in running. Rather than ending in a parking lot or expo space, you'll find yourself on a 19th-century ranch, in a bucolic setting, with a number of horse paddocks and a working blacksmith shop.

During the race, the park is closed to traffic. However, there's a firm 9:30 a.m. end time so that the park can reopen to visitors by 10 a.m. If you're lagging behind, you'll be on your own after the cutoff time.

Another unique and authentic aspect of this race is how generously it supports the community and the sport of running as a whole, especially for kids. Garden of the Gods is a not-for-profit operation, and a portion of its proceeds helps fund local high school track and cross-country teams. Grateful and enthusiastic students set up themed aid stations throughout the course. Station themes from past years have included a Hawaiian luau and an '80s hair band. After you finish the race, you can vote for your favorite themed station. The winners receive additional funds to cover a track or cross-country meet the school couldn't ordinarily attend. Whatever profits are left over from the race weekend go toward maintaining the trail system in the park.

KNOW BEFORE YOU GO

Running a race above 6,000 feet (1,800 m) of elevation isn't easy, especially if you live at or near sea level. Try to arrive a day or two early to give yourself time to acclimate, and drink plenty of fluids before, during, and after the race. But don't let the elevation scare you. Yes, you will likely feel fatigue sooner than usual, but if you adjust your pace and stay hydrated, you can still run a great race.

AROUND THE BAY ROAD RACE

A unique distance, a shoreline course, and unprecedented history

SEASON: Spring   **TOTAL NO. OF RUNNERS:** 6,000   **RACE DISTANCES:** 2K (3.2 mi); 5K; 10K; 15K; 30K (18.6 mi)
SURFACE: Paved roads   **DIFFICULTY:** Moderate

Around the Bay is the oldest footrace in North America. First run in 1894, three years before the first Boston Marathon (America's oldest annual marathon, page 112), the race has seen many iterations before arriving at today's peculiar 30K distance. There are very few 30K road races, and only one in this book. For many years, Around the Bay measured slightly more than 30.6 kilometers (19 mi). Then, in 1982, it settled on 30K. Why the change? Since its inception, the race had been closed to women. But throughout the 1970s, several female pioneers had been running an unofficial 30K race alongside the men. In 1979, organizers finally opened the race to women and made 30K the standard distance for all runners. Shorter distances of 2K, 5K, 10K, and 15K have been added in recent years to allow more runners to participate.

All of the races start in downtown Hamilton, which reminds me of my hometown of Bethlehem, Pennsylvania, the former home of Bethlehem Steel. Hamilton is still an active steel town, and both cities have smokestacks in their skylines, as well as hip new neighborhoods lined with cultural centers, bars, and restaurants. True to its name, Around the Bay's 30K course circumnavigates Hamilton Harbour, and the vast majority of the course is on or near the water, offering expansive views dotted with sailboats and ferries, and occasionally stiff winds. The March weather can be a mixed bag.

WHERE TO STAY

The Sheraton Hamilton is the largest hotel close to the race's start area. For nicer hotels and more varied nightlife, some runners stay in Toronto. But that means an hour-long drive into Hamilton on race morning, or you can take a train (about $12 Canadian and 50 minutes).

OPPOSITE: More than 3,400 runners completed the 2023 Around the Bay 30K.

PAGES 24-25: The course crosses the Burlington Canal Lift Bridge just before the 13-kilometer mark.

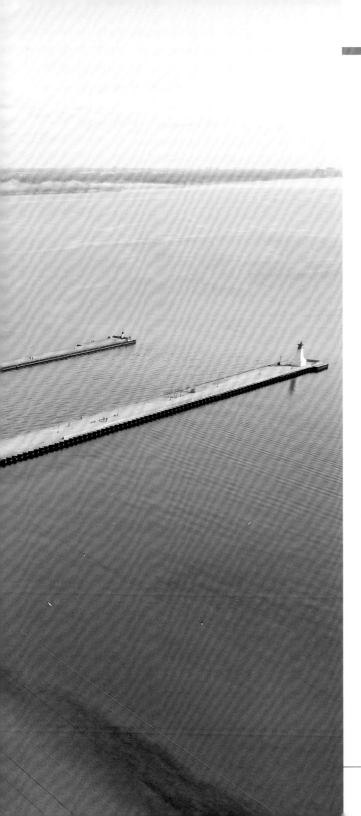

Plan to run in layers and be sure to pack some rain gear.

Near the halfway point, with the harbor on your left and the expanse of Lake Ontario to your right, you'll cross the Burlington Canal Lift Bridge and enter the relatively leafy burb of Burlington. There, you'll pass through crowds of cheering spectators at a golf course, LaSalle Park, and the Royal Botanical Gardens. Locals really embrace this event: Carry their enthusiasm with you! You'll need it around the 26-kilometer mark (16.2 mi), when you climb Valley Inn Hill. (You know it'll be challenging when a road's name has "hill" in it). You will now be above the harbor, having earned the course's best views and a descent back into downtown ... where Around the Bay's historically finicky distance has recently shifted again.

In 2024, the race's finish line was moved inside Tim Hortons Field, 2.5 miles (4 km) southeast of the 30K mark and home to Hamilton's two pro sports franchises (the Canadian Football League's Tiger-Cats and the Canadian Premier League's Forge FC soccer team). Runners now have the option of "laying up" at 30 kilometers, with a nod to tradition, or forging ahead through the extra miles to feel the glory of finishing inside a 23,000-seat sports landmark. Both the 30K and 34K marks have timing mats, and organizers report official results for both distances. Whether your "30K" race is 18.6 miles long or 21.1 is totally up to you!

BAY TO BREAKERS

A moving party with a huge field that's, well, clothing optional

SEASON: Late spring   **TOTAL NO. OF RUNNERS:** 20,000   **RACE DISTANCES:** 12K; 15K
SURFACE: Paved roads   **DIFFICULTY:** Challenging

You'll often hear races described as historic, and others promoted as being a big party. No race on Earth combines both accolades quite like Bay to Breakers. First run in 1912 to raise the spirits of a city still struggling from the earthquake of 1906, the race added a costume contest in the early '90s that, in true San Francisco spirit, has morphed into something a bit more progressive.

The race is among the largest in the world, and each year, hundreds (if not thousands) of participants run in all manner of costumes—from clowns and hula dancers to Marvel superheroes, Taylor Swifts, and Elvises (both early and late eras). But what makes this race truly distinctive are the many runners who wear nothing but a valid race bib and a pair of running shoes (and only the first is officially required). You see, nudity was allowed in San Francisco parks and public places until 2012. Keeping tradition alive, Bay to Breakers was among several long-held events exempted when public nudity was banned by the city. On race day, police just look the other way. Asked about the logistics of running au naturel, one runner told me he left his house naked, ran the race, hung out at the postrace party until he got cold, then came home. If you decide to don a costume, be sure to go all out. Don't just stick on some fake lamb-chop sideburns and call yourself Elvis—these runners mean business.

TRAVEL TIP

Lots of runners stay at the Hyatt Regency San Francisco, a short walk from the starting line. Postrace, you'll find lots of transportation options for returning to the Embarcadero area. Temperatures in San Francisco hover in the mid-60s Fahrenheit (around 18°C) in May. You'll want some extra clothes to stay warm after the race.

OPPOSITE: San Francisco's Alamo Square neighborhood features the "Painted Ladies," a row of colorful Victorian-style homes.

PAGES 28-29: These Where's Waldo? runners don't quite blend in with the race pack.

Bay to Breakers is more than the race's name. It's an identity and a vivid descriptor. The point-to-point course starts near the Embarcadero on the San Francisco Bay waterfront and winds west through the heart of the city before finishing at Ocean Beach on the Pacific Ocean. In 2023, organizers added a 15K, which includes a 1.9-mile (3 km) stretch along the Pacific on the Great Highway. Massive crowds line the challenging course the entire way. There's a steep climb (another San Francisco trademark) at the 2.5-mile (4 km) mark on Hayes Street, but the second half is quite flat, and the last few miles descend through picturesque Golden Gate Park.

Despite its size and festive atmosphere, Bay to Breakers hosts some of the fastest runners in the world. The course records for the 12K are 33:31 for men and 38:07 for women, both set by Kenyan runners. Even the Centipede Division (13 to 15 costumed runners who take on the entire race linked together by a bungee cord) features speedsters. The men's course record is 36:44, or a pace of 4:56 per mile. Impressive!

Inevitably, having a good time outweighs trying to run a fast time, and the race transforms into a raucous running party. In fact, the fun continues into the evening at the epic Finish Line Festival, which features live bands and sunset views over Ocean Beach.

BLOOMSDAY RUN

A quirky, iconic race with local color and one steep conquest

SEASON: **Spring**   TOTAL NO. OF RUNNERS: **30,000**   RACE DISTANCE: **12K**
SURFACE: **Paved roads**   DIFFICULTY: **Moderate**

Bloomsday started during the first running boom in 1977 as the brainchild of local legend and Olympic marathoner Don Kardong. That first year, 1,400 runners took on the course. By the mid-1990s, the race had more than 60,000 participants. Crowds have thinned a little since then to a still robust 30,000-plus, including a die-hard group of 71 runners called the Perennials who have completed all 48 Bloomsday races. How in the world has a 12K located in the northwest corner of the United States—where springtime weather can be finicky (to put it mildly)—become such a popular, iconic event?

Not because it's easy. The course starts downtown in Riverfront Park and winds along the Spokane River. Strong spectator support and multiple bands spur on runners, but a wake-up call arrives just before the five-mile (8 km) mark, where you'll encounter what's affectionately known as Doomsday Hill. Two-thirds of the way through the race, when fatigue often starts to set in, .72-mile-long (1.2 km) Doomsday rears with a 6.5 percent grade. It's not the toughest climb in this book, but the hype and mystique certainly can be intimidating. Be sure to pace yourself early in the race. Once you get a high five from the Doomsday Hill Vulture at the summit, you'll have smooth sailing back to Riverfront Park and the finish.

The Vulture, a costumed local named Bill Robinson who became the

OPPOSITE: Race by Washington Water Power's historic 19th-century plant, which overlooks iconic Spokane Falls.

PAGES 32-33: The elite wheelchair category is the first to leave the starting line on race weekend.

race's unofficial mascot in 1987 after creating the 10-foot-tall (3 m) costume for a Halloween contest, is one of many community-inspired quirks that really make this race worth doing. This town is passionate about running. Near the finish line, 40 life-size sculptures are all posed in running motion, as if the whole city is involved in the race. The locals, known as Spokanites, either run it, volunteer at it, or turn out to cheer on runners. Step into a neighborhood coffee shop, and if locals don't recognize you, they'll inevitably ask if you're in town for the race. Be ready for follow-up questions: *Where are you from? How many times have you run it? Did you high-five the Vulture?*

Unlike most races that give runners their T-shirts at registration, Bloomsday hands its shirts out as a reward *after* you cross the finish line. And this isn't your typical finisher's shirt. Every year, the race holds a competition for local artists to conceive the design. The winning artist receives a $1,000 prize, and runners head home with a coveted badge of honor.

WEATHER WATCH

In early May, Spokane's weather usually brings temperatures in the mid-30s Fahrenheit (1–2.5°C) at the start and in the 40s Fahrenheit (4–9°C) when you finish. (Other years, temps reach the 50s Fahrenheit [10–15°C].) This can be ideal for runners chasing fast times, or a little brisk for warm-weather birds. You can bundle up at the start and toss your gear into the treetops as you start moving. Everything left behind is collected and donated to charity—another great Bloomsday tradition.

BOLDER BOULDER

A Rocky Mountain epic with something for every runner

SEASON: Spring   **TOTAL NO. OF RUNNERS:** 40,000   **RACE DISTANCE:** 10K
SURFACE: Paved roads   **DIFFICULTY:** Moderate

Lots of races boast about having "something for everyone." This race truly does—world-class speedsters compete for prize money, competitive citizen runners chase PRs, beginners take part in their first big race. And I do mean big. Founded in 1979 with 2,700 runners, Bolder Boulder now has 40,000 participants, making it one of largest 10Ks in America.

As is common at races with so many runners, it goes off in waves rather than in a single mass start (which would be utter chaos). But Bolder Boulder does this uncommonly well, grouping runners into more than 100 waves. The first 30 to 40 waves are reserved for runners who will finish in under 75 minutes (a pace just over 12 minutes a mile). You must qualify for these waves by submitting an official time from a race during the prior calendar year. The first few qualified waves are filled with serious athletes going for the title of fastest citizen runners. The next 60 or so waves are open to anyone on a first-come, first-served basis. The last two waves are reserved for elites competing in the International Team Challenge, another Bolder Boulder trademark. Countries from all over the world can enter three-member teams in men's and women's fields that are scored cross-country style based on their finishing positions.

Perched in the foothills of the Rocky Mountains, 5,300 feet (1,615 m) above sea level, Boulder is a fitting locale for such an epic event. It's a mecca for endurance athletes looking to train at altitude. More than 100,000 spectators line the course, which winds through downtown, into shady neighborhoods,

OPPOSITE: Bolder Boulder's entrants include casual costumed racers and racing elites, and sometimes it's hard to tell the difference.

PAGES 36-37: Racers finish in a packed Folsom Field, where early waves gather to cheer on elites.

and, yes, up and down some tough hills before finishing on the University of Colorado's Folsom Field. This is where a unique vision—to gradually fill the stadium so that runners who've just finished can cheer on those who come in behind them—and Bolder Boulder's logistical excellence really pay off.

Because the elites start and finish last at Bolder Boulder, by the time they arrive, the stadium is absolutely packed. Imagine it: You've already earned your medal, and now you've got a catbird seat to watch the fastest runners in the world follow in your footsteps. You participate and then transform into a rabid fan, which connects you to the fabric of the race and to the sport at large. Some pros compare the atmosphere to the Olympics or the World Championships. It all culminates in one of the largest Memorial Day tributes in the country. Jets fly overhead, skydivers land on the field with flags for each branch of the U.S. military, and a group of enlistees take the oath to serve their country. Talk about a runner's high. I wish all races had a finish like this.

WHILE YOU'RE THERE

Given the altitude, it's wise to do at least one shakeout run before race day. Fortunately, there are more than 150 miles (240 km) of trails within the city limits. Among the most popular is the First and Second Flatirons Loop, a hilly 2.6-miler (4.2 km) with incredible views of the Rockies. The Boulder Creek Path, a mostly paved 5.5-mile (8.9 km) alternative that passes through downtown, is easier and more convenient.

CHERRY BLOSSOM 10 MILE RUN

A beautiful and wildly popular spring ritual for runners

SEASON: **Spring**   TOTAL NO. OF RUNNERS: **24,000**   RACE DISTANCES: **5K; 10 miles**
SURFACE: **Paved roads**   DIFFICULTY: **Easy**

It's human nature to rejoice when spring arrives, and among the best known (and most Instagram-worthy) celebrations of vernal giddiness in the United States is the National Cherry Blossom Festival in Washington, D.C. Several thousand cherry trees, a diplomatic gift from Japan, were planted near the Potomac River in the early 20th century. Every spring they transform into vivid clouds of pink, drawing more than 700,000 people to the nation's capital over a three-week span. So it's no surprise that the Cherry Blossom 10-miler is known as "the Runner's Rite of Spring." After all, runners are especially eager to turn the page on winter. Springtime brings the return of shorts, sunlight for those 6 a.m. training runs, and the exhilaration of a new racing season.

Kicking it off here really does feel special. The 10-mile loop course takes you past all the headliner monuments (Washington, Lincoln, and Jefferson), as well as the prime cherry blossom hot spots around the perimeter of the Tidal Basin (where 70 percent of the city's trees were planted) and along the National Mall. This part of the city is beautiful any time of year, but the blossoms give you the sense you're running inside a painting. Flowers drift through the air as though Mother Nature were tossing confetti to celebrate you and your fellow runners. The course is as flat as the Potomac—although the three-mile (4.8 km) leg out and around Hains Point gets windy. Unlike

TRAVEL TIP

Stay in the northwest quadrant of D.C. in or near the popular Georgetown neighborhood and all its restaurants, shops, and cafés. From there, you'll be about a mile (1.6 km)—an easy walk or rideshare—from the race's starting area. The Metro opens two hours early on Sunday, at 5 a.m., so runners can take the trains to the 10-miler start.

OPPOSITE: Cherry trees bloom around Washington, D.C.'s Tidal Basin in view of the Washington Monument.

PAGES 40-41: Runners make their way through the capital's National Mall.

most other big-city 10-milers, you don't run through a single neighborhood.

To be honest, the hardest part of this world-class event might be getting a bib. With more than 17,000 finishers, Cherry Blossom is so popular that the entry process is governed by a lottery system that begins four to five months prior to race day. You can sign up on the race's website to receive an alert when the lottery opens. If you don't get picked, consider volunteering instead. Race organizers usually accept 2,000 volunteers, who in turn are guaranteed entry into the following year's race. A 5K option on Saturday draws another 7,000 finishers and runs partly on Pennsylvania Avenue with the U.S. Capitol as a backdrop. If you're lucky and ambitious, you can sign up for the Double Blossom and do both.

If your goal is to run a fast time, arrive in D.C. at least a day early. Race weekend festivities include a terrific lineup of world-renowned inspirational speakers, best-selling authors, and panels with former race champions. You'll also have plenty of time to tour the monuments and cherry blossoms before race day. Trust me, it's easy to get distracted on this beautiful course!

CHARLESTON, SOUTH CAROLINA, U.S.A.

COOPER RIVER BRIDGE RUN

A Lowcountry point-to-point with a bridge to remember

SEASON: Spring **TOTAL NO. OF RUNNERS:** 40,000 **RACE DISTANCE:** 10K
SURFACE: Paved roads **DIFFICULTY:** Moderate

Point-to-point courses add logistical challenges you won't find at races that start and finish in the same area, so they're both less common and more limited in terms of race distances runners can choose from. On the other hand, point-to-points give organizers only one course and distance to manage, so they typically run like Swiss timepieces (aka to perfection). The Cooper River Bridge Run exemplifies all the above. Offering only a 10K, this race unfolds between Mount Pleasant and downtown Charleston. It also features an additional racing rarity—an epic bridge crossing.

The Lowcountry is known for its salt marshes, crooked waterways, and maritime forests of oak, Spanish moss, and palmetto trees. After starting in the town of Mount Pleasant, the course takes runners through and alongside the lush Lowcountry landscape before finishing in historic downtown Charleston. The first two miles (3.2 km) are flat, but then the Arthur Ravenel Jr. Bridge begins its gradual ascent over the Cooper River. The Ravenel Bridge is the longest cable-stayed bridge in North America, with a 2.5-mile (4 km) pedestrian path. If you gaze south toward Patriots Point, home of the Naval & Maritime Museum and the U.S.S. *Yorktown* (CV-10) aircraft carrier, you may not notice that you're running a hill. But the third mile is a steady climb, and the fourth a steady descent. That's bridge running in a nutshell. At its highest point, the bridge stands about 18 stories above the water. Although

OPPOSITE: If you're scared of heights, stick to the center lanes to avoid the stomach-dropping views as you cross the Cooper River.

PAGES 44-45: The Arthur Ravenel Jr. Bridge connects Mount Pleasant to downtown Charleston, and the views while crossing are worth the effort.

the Ravenel is quiet and peaceful, throngs of cheering spectators are there to greet you on the other side.

Prior to the span's opening in 2006, runners traversed the Silas N. Pearman Bridge, which employed a cantilever truss design with a suspended center span. Translation: You could feel the bridge move as you ran. It was terrifying! (But fitting of the longtime race slogan: "Get over it!") The Ravenel Bridge, thankfully, is a cable-stayed design with five spans that crest at 186 feet (57 m) above the river. When I crossed it, I didn't feel any movement. Runners who have a fear of heights told me it helped to run in the center lanes so they could look at their feet or straight ahead. Others with less vertigo will be rewarded with salt-tinged breezes and fantastic views.

The final two miles of the race are flat and fast, finishing in downtown Charleston with a warm welcome to the Bridge Run's massive, famous Finish Festival. Charleston is among America's greatest food cities, and I'm not sure I've seen more delicious options at any other finish line.

TRAVEL TIP

Choose to stay near the finish in Charleston's historic district or near the start in Mount Pleasant, known for its great restaurants, coffee shops, and beautiful parks. But here's where the point-to-point logistics kick in: One way or the other, you'll need to get from Charleston to Mount Pleasant (or vice versa). Fortunately, frequent bus and boat shuttles ferry runners where they need to go before and after the race.

CRESCENT CITY CLASSIC

Where flat and fast meet the Big Easy's Fat Tuesday

SEASON: Spring   **TOTAL NO. OF RUNNERS:** 20,000   **RACE DISTANCE:** 10K
SURFACE: Paved roads   **DIFFICULTY:** Easy

Nicknamed "A Race for All Y'all," the Crescent City Classic is an Easter Saturday tradition with 20,000 runners filling the streets of the Big Easy. Given that roughly 50 percent of New Orleans is below sea level, this point-to-point, lightning-fast course is among the flattest in the United States. The race starts in front of the Superdome, home of the NFL's Saints, before turning toward historic Jackson Square, the French Quarter, coffee-and-beignet treasure Café Du Monde, and the welcome shade of ancient live oak trees with their gobs of Spanish moss. Just past the New Orleans Museum of Art lies the raucous finish line in City Park.

The weather can be warm and humid, with highs in the mid-70s Fahrenheit (around 24°C) and lows in the 50s Fahrenheit (10–15°C). The 8 a.m. start helps, but dehydration can be an issue. Organizers know this and offer plenty of well-stocked aid stations throughout the course, as well as a vehicle trailing the field that can transport anyone who can't continue to the finish.

In a town whose other signature events include Mardi Gras and Jazz Fest, it's no surprise that the Crescent City's finish-line spread, called RaceFest, is a capital-*P* Party. That means authentic N'awlins bands, food, and drinks (and not just the electrolyte variety). At some races, finishers pause just long enough to grab something to eat on the way back to their hotels. It's not unusual for people to sign up for Crescent City just for the party—which

WHERE TO STAY

The Hyatt Regency New Orleans is just a block away from the starting line and within easy walking distance of great restaurants and cafés. It also hosts the two-day Health & Fitness Expo, which makes for hassle-free packet pickup. Wherever you stay, reserve early: Mardi Gras ends just before Easter and booking will be competitive.

Crescent City Classic racers will run past St. Louis Cathedral in Jackson Square in New Orleans.

ABOVE: RaceFest attendees greet every runner (or walker) at the finish line.

OPPOSITE: The Crescent City Classic's charity program aims to fundraise $1 million every year for organizations such as the local Bastion Community of Resilience, a nonprofit that supports injured veterans and their families.

is open to the public for $20 a head, a good deal in return for top-notch gumbo and jambalaya.

Also fitting with the Mardi Gras vibe, lots of people run in costumes. You'll see everything from tutu-wearing fairies to Zulu warriors. And, of course, lots of beaded necklaces. The fun has a good cause behind it too: The Run For It program sets out to raise $1 million each year to support two dozen local charities selected by the nonprofit Crescent City Fitness Foundation. Runners (and walkers) agree to raise at least $200 for the partner charity of their choice and get a unique fundraising page and discounted registration fee. If they raise $300, their full registration fee is refunded.

If you can't make it to New Orleans, the Race for All Y'all has an option to run the race virtually. Runners who submit a DIY 10K result to the race's app receive a finisher's T-shirt and medal ... but they have to throw their own party.

EMPIRE STATE BUILDING RUN-UP

An iconic challenge fitting of the world-famous skyscraper

SEASON: Fall   **TOTAL NO. OF RUNNERS:** 300–400   **RACE DISTANCE:** 86 flights (about 0.2 mi/320 m)
SURFACE: Concrete   **DIFFICULTY:** Challenging

This quite simply is unlike any other race in the world, and there's nothing simple about it. Running up the stairwell of the Empire State Building—86 floors and 1,576 steps—was the most grueling 14 minutes and 30 seconds of my life. The fastest runners finish the task in around 10 minutes. Weekend warriors take 20 to 25 minutes, and the back of the pack finishes in around an hour.

Here's a tip: If you can train in an actual stairwell, it will help. The next best option is a StairMaster. And dial in your technique. If you need to hit every step, work on building a fast turnover so you climb quickly. If you have a longer stride and can cover two steps at a time, do that instead (I found early in the race I could cover two steps per stride, but toward the top of the building, I was hitting every step anyway). You can use the handrail to keep your balance—and even propel yourself forward.

Spectators are prohibited in the stairwell, but you'll find lots of camaraderie among the participants, who cheer one another on and call out "On your left!" while passing. About halfway through the climb—around the 43rd floor or so—you have a few dozen feet of flat ground before you switch to a stairwell on the other side of the building. The stairwell is dry and dusty, and temperatures can reach 80°F (26.6°C). But that just makes the finish line on the top-floor observatory of this iconic building feel even more epic.

KNOW BEFORE YOU GO

Wear padded cycling gloves for the handrail and never look at what floor you're on. The stairwell doors are marked with the floor number, but stay focused on the steps. I looked once and expected to see the number 30. I was only on number 10.

By floor 20 of the Empire State Building Run-Up, most runners are feeling the burn. Only 66 floors to go!

FALMOUTH ROAD RACE

A fast and famous classic on the Atlantic Ocean

SEASON: Summer   **TOTAL NO. OF RUNNERS:** 11,000   **RACE DISTANCE:** 7 miles (11 km)
SURFACE: Paved roads   **DIFFICULTY:** Moderate

Up around Cape Cod, the eastward-protruding peninsula that gives Massachusetts its arm-flexing coastal shape, a summertime rule of thumb states that once you're on the Cape, you never leave the Cape. After I finished my first Falmouth Road Race, I spoke to lots of Cape Codders near the finish line and asked them what was next on their racing schedule. I got the same response from everyone: "We only run races on the Cape." For more than 50 years, thousands of mainlanders have traveled Capeward every August to join them, lured by one of the best races in the United States.

The Falmouth Road Race originated when local runner and philanthropist Tommy Leonard, inspired by Frank Shorter winning the gold medal in the 1972 Olympic marathon, founded the race to help the Falmouth Track Club raise funds for high school girls competing in meets. To this day, the charity program bolsters the event. Shorter himself joined the race in its third year for the first of his many Falmouths (he won it twice), and it still draws an impressive elite field.

As you might expect from a 50-year-old race held in a sleepy, hard-to-reach locale, tradition reigns. The iconic race begins in front of the Captain Kidd restaurant in the historic village of Woods Hole, once known for whaling and fishing but now a hub of tourism and marine research. After passing Nobska Lighthouse and tracing Vineyard Sound, the course finishes by the beach in Falmouth Heights. Essentially, you run from one type of watering hole to another—which makes sense, as Tommy Leonard was also a

TRAVEL TIP

Traffic is intense on the island, so try to arrive a couple days early and make a summer vacation out of it. Old Silver Beach is a popular spot in Falmouth. Or take the 30-minute ferry ride to the numerous beaches on Martha's Vineyard. Rent a bike and ride the Shining Sea Bikeway, a paved 10.7-mile (17.2 km) path that hugs the coastline between Woods Hole and Falmouth.

Nobska Lighthouse sits near mile marker 1.

ABOVE: By 1978, Falmouth was attracting elites (former American marathon record holder Bill Rodgers won that year's race)—and thousands of fans to watch them compete.

OPPOSITE: The Captain Kidd restaurant has been the official starting point of the event since the first race in 1973.

bartender—cheered on by 75,000 spectators. The race has grown significantly since its inception, but it caps out at 11,000 people each year. Demand far exceeds that, so unless you're a Falmouth resident, you'll need to enter a lottery in early May and hope to get a number.

If you do, be sure to train in the heat and on some hills. It gets hot and humid out on the Cape in August, and temperatures can change significantly on race morning. It was warm the year I ran the race. Fortunately, we had a cool breeze coming off Vineyard Sound.

The first three miles (4.8 km) include seven different climbs. The next three and a half miles (5.6 km) are flat, with beautiful views of the sound—but one last steep hill awaits before the finish line. Look for the massive American flag waving runners in and let the downhill carry you across.

GASPARILLA DISTANCE CLASSIC

Two days, four races, and plenty of chances to party

SEASON: Winter   **TOTAL NO. OF RUNNERS: 30,000**   **RACE DISTANCES: 5K; 8K (5 mi); 15K; half-marathon**
SURFACE: Paved roads   **DIFFICULTY: Easy**

"Distance classic" is a nostalgia-tinged label for a series of races between a 5K and a marathon that are part of the same event. The Gasparilla Distance Classic, founded in 1978, is a two-day celebration of four races totaling more than 30 miles (48 km). Fresh on the heels of Gasparilla Pirate Fest, the event is named after the mythical pirate José "Gasparilla" Gaspar. Many of the "pirates" that invade the festival (at least those who run) stick around for race weekend and get some extra wear out of their costumes on the course, adding a unique swashbuckling atmosphere to the proceedings. Gasparilla is the only race I've been to where a common cheer is "ARRGGHH! Shiver me timbers!"

When I first ran it back in the late 1980s, the race consisted of just a 5K and a 15K. The longer race attracted a world-class field of elite runners vying for prize money, while the 5K was a nice addition for runners of all skill levels. Nobody had the idea of running both events back then, but at some point, it became popular to run multiple races in one weekend. Today, Gasparilla accommodates multitaskers by staggering the start times for each distance, making it possible to register for a "challenge" and run two, three, or even four races over two days. (In 2010, Gasparilla added a marathon, known as the "Final Voyage." I ran it, but apparently another 26.2 miles was a lot to ask of runners—that was the last year Gasparilla hosted a marathon distance.)

TRAVEL TIP

For beach options, consider Clearwater and St. Pete Beach within a half-hour drive of downtown Tampa. After a day in the sun, head to the historic Ybor City neighborhood for terrific Cuban and Latin restaurants.

OPPOSITE: The Hillsborough River cuts its way through downtown Tampa.

PAGES 58-59: Runners cross the starting line for the Gasparilla 8K.

The festivities begin on Saturday with the 15K, which draws more than 4,000 participants and is still regarded as the event's signature race. The 5K—the largest race of the weekend with 8,000 entrants who range from speedsters to walkers to moms and dads with strollers—starts about two and a half hours later. In 2021, a participant named Betty Ashley walked the 5K a few months prior to her 100th birthday. Accompanied by lots of family members, she crossed the finish line and inspired the entire Tampa community.

The half-marathon kicks off Sunday morning, and like the 15K it starts in the predawn half-light, treating runners to a stunning sunrise over the bay. The 8K begins three and a half hours afterward.

All four races feature out-and-back courses that unfold entirely (or at least mostly) on Bayshore Boulevard, a four-lane thoroughfare on the shore of Hillsborough Bay with postcard-worthy views of downtown Tampa. (The half-marathon takes a four-mile [6.4 km] detour in its

WEATHER WATCH

The gap in starting times between the longer races and their shorter follow-ups can make for unpredictable conditions—temps in the 40s and 50s Fahrenheit (4–15°C) in the morning but warm enough by the afternoon for a jump in the pool. Be prepared to hydrate and adjust your pace if conditions call for it. There are aid stations at every mile, as well as four sprinkler showers on Bayshore Boulevard.

early parts through the tony neighborhoods on Davis Islands before rejoining Bayshore.) These courses are flat and fast—the very definition of sea level—and they still attract top professionals. The half-marathon course records were set in 2015 by U.S. Olympians Dathan Ritzenhein (1:03:16) and Jen Rhines (1:12:34). Recent winners haven't been quite as quick, but the men still run sub-1:10 and the women finish around 1:20. For those who aren't in it for speed, there's also a stroller roll 5K and a walking 5K wave.

Postrace celebrations and awards ceremonies on both Saturday and Sunday feature ice-cold towels that feel so good they should be standard-issue at every warm-weather event. If you're considering one of the two-day challenges, perhaps the idea of two parties with happy, sweaty pirates will nudge you off the fence.

ABOVE: Australian shepherd Roxie finished the Gasparilla 15K as a service dog.

OPPOSITE: Inclusivity is a key of the Gasparilla, where this 5K wheelchair competitor sprints toward the finish.

MANCHESTER ROAD RACE

A truly unique holiday tradition (and preemptive calorie burn)

SEASON: Fall (Thanksgiving Day)   **TOTAL NO. OF RUNNERS: 10,000**   **RACE DISTANCE: 4.748 miles (7.6 km)**
SURFACE: Paved roads   **DIFFICULTY: Easy**

Maybe it's the anticipation of vast caloric intake. Perhaps it's the cool, crisp weather that makes for ideal race conditions. Or it could just be a simple desire to gather with like-minded folks for a shared gesture of gratitude and celebration. Whatever the reasons, more runners finish road races on Thanksgiving Day than on any other day of the year (including the Fourth of July, which held this distinction until 2012). Most of these participants are running small, hyperlocal turkey trots, but a big swath—10,000 these days but historically as many as 15,000—are running the granddaddy of 'em all: the Manchester Road Race.

First run in 1927, Manchester is among the most joyfully traditionbound races in the United States, starting with its odd and anachronistic distance of 4.748 miles. A more modern race would undoubtedly stretch things out to a more standard five miles or even 10K. But Manchester decided to keep with tradition and stuck with the unique length its founders laid out almost 100 years ago. The course begins and ends on Main Street, naturally, starting at the civil but unorthodox time of 10 a.m. And in this inflationary age, organizers charge what sounds like a throwback promotional fee for an entry: just $32. This might be the best bargain in running. But the race fills up quickly, so sign up early. Registration typically opens at the beginning of September.

TRAVEL TIP

Many participants drive from other parts of New England on race day, which means traffic will be heavy. If you're traveling from outside the area, Bradley International Airport outside Hartford has lots of connecting flights and is only a half-hour drive to Manchester.

OPPOSITE: Eventual winner Nick Willis of New Zealand leads the pack through falling snow during the 2005 edition of the Manchester Road Race.

PAGES 64–65: The 2018 race day had clear skies, and thousands of runners packed Main Street.

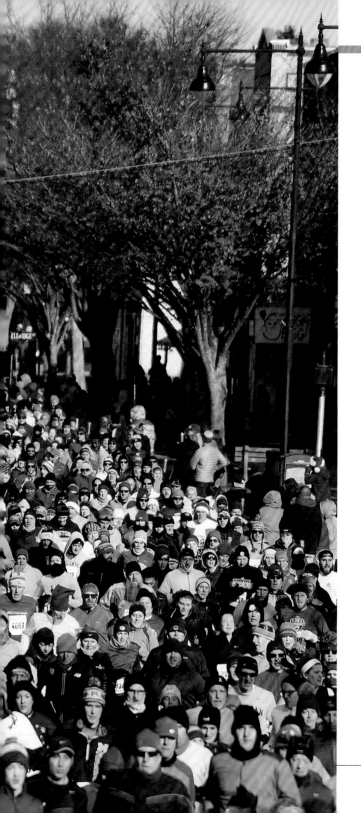

The course, which is flat and fast, traces a big loop around town. The streets are lined with cheering locals, some with a cup of coffee, others taking it up a notch with a full-on tailgate. There's only one hill, but a race within the race—common in cycling but rare in running—keeps it interesting: The first male and female to reach the summit near the two-mile (3.2 km) mark win a $1,000 cash prize and, at least for a year, are crowned King and Queen of the Hill.

Although the race attracts plenty of elites chasing that honor (and other prize money), its biggest celebrities are runners who've made Manchester part of their own traditions "for an exemplary number of years." Organizers maintain a Longevity Table recognizing those who have run Manchester 25 times or more, and these Perennial Performers are given special red-white-and-blue race bibs. Amazingly, two men have run Manchester more than 60 times, and a pair of women have run at least 50. (Like many historic races, Manchester was closed to women until the 1970s.)

One of those Perennial Performers is Amby Burfoot, who won the race nine times and finished his 61st in 2023. "After I stopped finishing near the top," he says, "I continued running it every year because I believe running is more important as a lifetime pursuit than a competitive quest." Words to live by—and perhaps some inspiration to start a Thanksgiving tradition of your own.

MONUMENT AVENUE 10K

An organizational marvel and a jaunt through modern history

SEASON: **Spring**   TOTAL NO. OF RUNNERS: **25,000**   RACE DISTANCES: **1 mile; 10K**
SURFACE: **Paved roads**   DIFFICULTY: **Easy**

First things first: the name. For more than a century, Monument Avenue featured a procession of monuments to Confederate figures, including Stonewall Jackson, Jefferson Davis, and Robert E. Lee, whose 60-foot-tall (18 m) statue was a focal point of Richmond, the former capital of the Confederacy. In 2020 and 2021, however, all of the area's Civil War–era statues were removed. The traffic circle where Lee's monument stood is now home to more than 6,000 plants and 28 trees. Monument Avenue, however, has retained its name, and its last remaining statue honors Arthur Ashe, the late tennis champion and civil rights advocate who was born, raised, and buried in Richmond.

The Monument Avenue 10K, first run in 2000, remains as distinctive and popular as ever. Its out-and-back course is flat and fast, with two quick turns right after the start before runners hit the race's namesake road. Then they cruise down two parallel three-mile (4.8 km) straightaways with a hairpin turn in between. If that sounds boring, it's anything but. For one thing, this is a spectacularly beautiful course. Those parallel straightaways are separated by a verdant grass median, and Monument Avenue—formally designated an Old and Historic Neighborhood—is lined with massive shade trees, cherry blossoms (usually in bloom on race day), and colonial-style homes and churches.

WHILE YOU'RE THERE

Belle Isle, a 54-acre (22 ha) park in the middle of the James River, is a great destination for a three- to four-mile (4.8–6.4 km) shakeout run. From Monroe Park, run under the Robert E. Lee Bridge along a suspended walkway. On the other side is a single-track path around the perimeter of the island, right along the river, with views of Richmond's skyline.

You won't be starved for fantastic real estate sights on Richmond's Monument Avenue.

ABOVE: Plenty of high school runners and young athletes dot the field of competitors.

OPPOSITE: Local marching bands offer musical motivation for runners on the out-and-back course.

The route is also lined with dozens of bands, DJs, cheer zones, and porch parties—by far the most entertainment I've ever experienced on a 10K course. Some races market themselves as having a band every mile, but here there seems to be one on every block. This creates an upbeat, festive atmosphere in keeping with Richmond's running scene: Sports Backers, the nonprofit that puts on the race, has a goal of making Richmond the most physically active community in the United States.

The first race of the day is the 10K Mini, a one-mile race for kids aged four to 12. More than 1,000 kids enter, and local schools have running programs to help them train for the big day. Some burgeoning overachievers finish the mini and then also head out to conquer the 10K.

You'll find lots of good food and live music at the postrace festival in Monroe Park, where the party goes on for hours.

MOUNT WASHINGTON ROAD RACE

Where there is quite literally nowhere to go but up (and up)

SEASON: Summer   **TOTAL NO. OF RUNNERS:** 1,000   **RACE DISTANCE:** 7.6 miles (12.2 km)
SURFACE: Paved roads   **DIFFICULTY:** Extremely challenging

This epic event's slogan is "There's Only One Hill." Technically, it's true. But the hill in question—Mount Washington—is the highest peak in the northeastern United States, towering 6,288 feet (1,917 m) above sea level. Even the winners take about an hour to cover the 7.6 miles to the peak. The course follows the Mount Washington Auto Road, and aside from a short stretch at the beginning, every single step goes up. The total vertical gain from start to finish is 4,650 feet (1,420 m), with an average gradient of 12 percent (the max setting on many treadmills). I still remember the final 50 yards (46 m). It was like running up a wall, with its 22 percent gradient.

You start amid an emerald canopy of trees but finish well above the tree line. And you must dress for the conditions, because Mount Washington has another slogan: "Home of the World's Worst Weather." That can mean heavy rain, fog, lightning storms, and—most especially—heavy winds. The average annual wind speed is 35 miles an hour (56 km/h), and both the highest wind speed ever recorded in the United States (250 miles an hour [402 km/h]) and the coldest windchill ever recorded in the world (minus 108°F [−77.8°C]) occurred at the summit.

Fortunately, race organizers really know what they're doing. With the exception of 2020, when, like most races, it was canceled by the COVID-19 pandemic, the race has been run every year since 1936. Organizers constantly

ENTERING THE RACE

A lottery for entrants opens in February for this limited race. However, 200 slots are reserved on a first-come, first-served basis in January for charity runners who commit to raise $200. A small number of elites and certified Mountain Goats (those who have finished the required number of courses on the official USATF–New England Mountain Circuit) can qualify.

Runners make their way above the clouds to the peak of Mount Washington.

monitor weather conditions on top of the mountain, and if it's not safe, you won't run. In any case, you should prepare for anything. It could be 60°F (15.6°C) and sunny at the starting line and then 30°F (−1.1°C) and snowing at the finish. Dress for the top of the mountain.

You'll need to prearrange a ride off the top of the mountain. Most runners enlist support drivers, who are allowed to park at the summit. Some hardy souls walk or run back down, but you should only consider this if you have warm clothing with you.

Finally, pacing this race is key to finishing. Shorten your stride length and maintain a faster cadence than you would on flat ground. You'll want to lean forward into the incline, but don't bend at the waist. And to avoid getting psyched out, turn the advice commonly given to people with acrophobia on its head: Don't look up!

ABOVE: **Climb your way to the finish—and epic views above the clouds.**

OPPOSITE: **Prepare for an ascent: Mount Washington is the tallest peak in the northeastern United States.**

PEACHTREE ROAD RACE

A race that boasts that big-city feel without a big-time commitment

SEASON: Summer (Fourth of July) **TOTAL NO. OF RUNNERS:** 60,000 **RACE DISTANCE:** 10K
SURFACE: Paved roads **DIFFICULTY:** Moderate

Every runner's bucket list should include at least one epic big-city race. These typically feature 50,000 to 60,000 runners of all abilities, from world-class elites to first-timers; lots of pomp and circumstance; goose bump–giving crowds of spectators; and closed courses kept safe by a small army of officials and volunteers. By definition, these races are held in vibrant, diverse urban centers teeming with hotels, restaurants, and cultural experiences to enjoy while you're in town. After finishing one of these races, you can wear your medal proudly in public without feeling the least bit self-conscious, because everyone else is wearing theirs too. It's a beautiful thing when runners take over a city like this, and the city not only welcomes them but *embraces* them.

Normally, you need to run a marathon or half-marathon to have this type of big-city experience. But the Peachtree Road Race, which was founded in Atlanta in 1970 and bills itself as the largest 10K in the world, delivers on all counts without requiring quite as much training or racing commitment from runners. Held every Fourth of July and put on by the Atlanta Track Club—one of the largest and most diverse running clubs in the United States, with more than 30,000 members—Peachtree has become a bucket-list race for runners from around the world, attracting 60,000 every year and cementing the race's place as a cultural pillar of the city.

WHILE YOU'RE THERE

Visit Phidippides, the "original specialty running store," located on Piedmont Avenue in Midtown. Founded in 1973 by Jeff Galloway, an Atlanta native who won the first Peachtree in 1970 and ran the 1972 Olympic marathon, the shop carries anything you might need for the race.

OPPOSITE: Everything about Peachtree—one of the largest races in the world—is *big,* including the crowd of competitors.
PAGES 76-77: Visit Lake Clara Meer for a shakeout run— you'll find this dogwood sculpture and skyline views along the water's edge.

In Hotlanta, July 4 sounds like imperfect timing for an endurance event. When I ran this race in the 1990s, the heat was tolerable, but other years the humidity has laid runners low. Be prepared. You can acclimate to the conditions by doing a few lunchtime training runs in the weeks leading up to the race. Make sure you hydrate.

Most big-city races host health and fitness expos, and Peachtree's, held at the Georgia World Congress Center, is both massive and enjoyable. You'll need to swing by to pick up your race bib, but don't expect a race T-shirt—at least not yet. Peachtree's tee is one of the most coveted pieces of race swag in running. Every year, artists are invited to submit a design, which is put to a public vote online. Though most races give out their shirts prior to the start, Peachtree has the tradition of granting T-shirts only to finishers, as bragging rights. As a result, one of the expo's traditions is peacocking around in a race shirt from a prior year. Big bragging rights are in order if you have one of the finisher shirts from the 1970s.

Peachtree also has a notably large contingent of wheelchair racers. The Shepherd Center

KNOW BEFORE YOU GO

If you're in town with family, the Peachtree Junior is held on July 3 in Piedmont Park. It's free to all kids and features a timed mile that ends at the 10K finish line of the big race, meant to give kids aged six to 14 a big-city experience of their own. There's also a 50-meter dash for kids six and under. Piedmont Park is a beautiful, shady venue for a three- to four-mile (4.8–6.4 km) shakeout run before or after the 10K.

hospital, located between miles three and four on the course, focuses on rehabilitation for people with spinal cord injuries and is host to a dedicated wheelchair division. These athletes are impressive—they can cover the 10K course in under 20 minutes!

The point-to-point course starts uptown in the upscale Buckhead neighborhood, which looks and feels like a small city unto itself. After two quick climbs, Peachtree Road descends slowly for a few miles on its way back downtown. The toughest stretch is Cardiac Hill near the three-mile mark. Fortunately, one of the course's seven live bands sets up at its base to give you a boost for the climb. Everything's going to feel like a breeze from there, especially with the crowds cheering you on—some 150,000 spectators turn out on race day. A big postrace celebration happens in Piedmont Park, where you'll get your finisher medal and, finally, that coveted shirt.

ABOVE: Thousands of volunteers serve Peachtree's runners.

OPPOSITE: It takes a lot of energy to motivate 60,000 participants. Spirit groups, bands, and DJs apply to line the course.

PART TWO

MARATHONS

Runners race past the Louvre during the Schneider Electric Marathon de Paris (page 202).

BIG SUR INTERNATIONAL MARATHON

A race with iconic views of the Pacific coast

SEASON: Spring   **NO. OF MARATHON RUNNERS:** 4,500   **OTHER RACE DISTANCES:** 5K; 12K; 11 miles (17.7 km); 21 miles (33.8 km); marathon relay   **ELEVATION GAIN/LOSS:** 2,182 feet (665 m)/2,528 feet (771 m)   **DIFFICULTY:** Challenging

If you run only one marathon race in your life, the Big Sur International Marathon is an obvious choice. The route is one of the most visually stunning in the world, following California State Route 1 along the Pacific Ocean from the hamlet of Big Sur north to the finish line in the eclectic village of Carmel.

The race begins on a gentle downhill, under a canopy of redwood trees—the tallest trees in the world, growing 300 feet (90 m) high or more—which provide five miles (8 km) of welcome shade and cool, crisp air (the temperatures on race day average between 50° and 60°F [10–16°C]). At mile six, that grand protective forest gives way to lush green meadows, cow pastures, and mountains flanking the right side of the highway. By mile eight, when the ocean comes into view, runners encounter the two biggest challenges of the course: hills and headwind. These elements can throw off your pace per mile and hijack an otherwise awe-inspiring experience, so instead, run your race according to your perceived effort. You might slow down, but running Big Sur is much more about relishing the views than it is about clocking a personal record. This is a difficult marathon course.

Between miles 10 and 12, runners face a steep uphill measuring more than 500 feet (150 m) to the highest destination on the course, called Hurricane Point. The race's famed *taiko* drummers pound their instruments at the base

GETTING AROUND

Race organizers at Big Sur offer bus transportation from several hotels in Monterey to the starting line. Taking the race-sanctioned transportation is mandatory because Highway 1 is closed to all other traffic on race morning.

OPPOSITE: You'll run your way past sand dunes and tall beach grass, which make Big Sur as scenic as it is challenging.

PAGES 84-85: The Bixby Bridge—one of the most photographed bridges in California—marks the halfway point of the marathon.

to motivate your climb (try running to the beat!). The halfway point of the race is at hand after cresting that hill—and it's a sight you might remember forever: the Bixby Bridge, a concrete architectural marvel with its grand arch 260 feet (80 m) above the canyon carved by Bixby Creek. Each year, a Yamaha grand piano sits at the end of the bridge, where a local pianist plays inspirational tunes until the very last runner has passed. The scene is so breathtaking, some marathoners have stopped to make marriage proposals before continuing on to Carmel.

By mile 22, participants near the town of Carmel and enjoy more crowd support from residents who come out to cheer along the streets of the Carmel Highlands. Locals have been known to throw quite a party at the Chevron station, with live music and kids handing out berries to runners. The entirety of the course is closed to vehicles and bikes, so the return to civilization is a treat for those looking for a morale boost. The not-so-good news is that the terrain does not flatten out until mile 24, just before the

APRÈS RACE

While the race itself gives visitors a comprehensive tour of one of the most gorgeous landscapes in the world, the region offers plenty of other opportunities to explore. Give your legs a break on a whale-watching cruise. Many of these tours take off from Fisherman's Wharf in Monterey, which also offers seafood dining options and shopping.

route passes Point Lobos State Natural Reserve (bookmark Point Lobos for a gentle hike in the days after the race). The reserve is the "greatest meeting of land and water in the world," according to early 1900s landscape painter Francis McComas, and is home to sea lions, orcas, harbor seals, and more.

One significant ascent, about a quarter mile (0.4 km) in length, remains in the final mile. After enduring that last sneaky climb, the sweet reward that follows the finish line comes in the form of hot soup, more live music, and a beer garden, which all help jump-start a well-deserved celebration.

This race has a long history, including its record finishing times. The course record for men is 2:16:39, achieved by Brad Hawthorne in 1987; for women, the record was set by Svetlana Vasilyeva in 1996, at 2:41:34. Maybe you're up for the challenge of breaking one of these 20-year-plus records.

ABOVE: **There's no greater joy than crossing the finish line proudly.**

OPPOSITE: **A pianist greets all those who survive Hurricane Point.**

ATHENS AUTHENTIC MARATHON

A historic race inspired by Pheidippides himself

SEASON: Fall   **NO. OF MARATHON RUNNERS: 20,000**   **OTHER RACE DISTANCES: 5K; 10K**
ELEVATION GAIN/LOSS: 1,258 feet (383 m)/1,097 feet (334 m)   **DIFFICULTY: Challenging**

Legend has it that during the Battle of Marathon between the Athenians and the Persians in 490 B.C., Pheidippides ran from the city of Marathon to Athens (a distance of about 25 miles, or 40 kilometers) to deliver the message that the Persians had been defeated. Then, the story goes, he immediately died of exhaustion. Today, more than a million people run the same distance each year—without the fatal ending. In fact, at the first Olympics in 1896, competitors followed Pheidippides' route, giving birth to the modern-day marathon, though it's now a bit longer, at a standard distance of 26.2 miles (42.2 km).

The legend lives on at the Athens Authentic Marathon, held each November on roughly the same course that Pheidippides is believed to have run thousands of years ago, though the hilly roads are paved now. Most international participants choose to make a vacation out of the annual event (the race lists its official travel agency partners on its website), staying in Athens for the sightseeing opportunities. The race organization and marathon tour companies that organize the trips for out-of-towners arrange bus service on race morning from various points in Athens to the start in Marathon, a small coastal town of about 8,000 residents. Many racers, therefore, opt for one of the many hotels near the finish line at Panathenaic Stadium, the marble arena dubbed "the birthplace of the modern Olympic Games."

OPPOSITE: The Acropolis dominates the skyline of Athens.

PAGES 90-91: What a finish! The race ends in the Panathenaic Stadium, originally opened in 566 B.C. and the only stadium in the world built entirely of marble.

Runners begin on a flat stretch of road that takes them past Marathon Tomb, the burial site of Greek soldiers who died in the Battle of Marathon. The beginning and end of the run are packed with history, while the middle portion features grueling hills. The ascent begins around kilometer 18 and doesn't relent until around kilometer 32. The good news is that it's mostly downhill to the finish from there. Word to the wise: Prepare by running plenty of uphill *and* downhill. Your quads will suffer in those last seven miles (11 km) if you haven't trained for the pounding of a gradual descent.

Though the main draw might be the chance to experience Pheidippides' journey for yourself, plenty of attractions await in Athens. Looking for a place to take your shakeout run? Head to the 500-meter track on the rim of the Panathenaic Stadium, where you'll enjoy views of the Acropolis and Lycabettus Hill (go early, before the path becomes crowded with tourists). Or head to the National Garden in the city center, where you'll run among century-old trees and ancient Greek columns.

APRÈS RACE

What better way to unwind than by heading to the beach? The Greek Islands are a must-see, and they offer many scenic runs for those who wish to add some adventures on foot. Many of the tour companies that arrange travel for the race also organize such excursions. Crete, a favorite, is the largest of the islands and offers stunning traffic-free trails along the crystal blue seas.

ABOVE: Elites from around the globe flock to the grounds of the first Olympics.

OPPOSITE: This sculpture—known as "Dromeas," or "The Runner"—urges marathoners along the final mile of the race.

Of course, you'll need to fuel (and refuel) for race day. Don't leave Greece without feasting on souvlaki, a pita stuffed with marinated meat, tomato, and onion; or spanakopita, a savory pie made of phyllo dough and filled with spinach and feta cheese. Athens has a vibrant street food culture, and easy-to-find casual places serve delicious Greek cuisine. If you're hoping to toast your marathon finish, look for rooftop establishments that feature views of the ancient ruins and stunning sunsets.

TRAINING TIP

The Athens Authentic Marathon is among the hilliest of races. The long, gradual ascent in the middle of the race takes some physical and mental preparation. Make sure that at least one of your training runs each week incorporates a hilly route. If you live in a flat area, try getting on a treadmill and utilizing the incline.

AUCKLAND MARATHON

Enjoy the "good on ya" spirit of the Kiwis.

SEASON: Southern Hemisphere spring   **NO. OF MARATHON RUNNERS:** 2,000   **OTHER RACE DISTANCES:** 5K; 11K (6.8 mi); half-marathon   **ELEVATION GAIN/LOSS:** 712 feet (217 m)/711 feet (216 m)   **DIFFICULTY:** Moderate

Many runners start race day by taking the ferry from Auckland, across the harbor, to the starting line in Devonport, a scenic suburb. The 12-minute ride offers one of the best vantage points to see the Auckland skyline. The race itself begins with rolling hills until about kilometer nine and then flattens out considerably as the course traces the waterfront—which is not only easier on the legs but also provides a chance to distract yourself with views of the harbor. A highlight is cruising over the Auckland Harbour Bridge, which joins St. Mary's Bay with Northcote, where a local drumming group motivates everybody from elites to those keeping an eye on things from the rear.

No trip to Auckland is complete without getting at least one bird's-eye view of the vast waterways and lush green landscapes. After race day, take a short hike up Mount Eden, the highest volcanic peak in the area, or visit the observation deck at Sky Tower, the second tallest freestanding structure in the Southern Hemisphere. If hobbits are your thing, book a tour of the Hobbiton Movie Set, the location of Peter Jackson's film trilogy. Don't forget to treat yourself to hokey pokey after the race—that's New Zealand's favorite ice cream flavor, consisting of vanilla ice cream with sprinkles of honeycomb toffee. You can toast your 26.2-mile accomplishment with a glass of New Zealand's famous sauvignon blanc.

Most athletes hop on an early ferry to reach the Auckland Marathon starting line in Devonport.

BARCELONA MARATHON

A route made for setting records and seeing the city

SEASON: Spring **NO. OF MARATHON RUNNERS:** 20,000 **OTHER RACE DISTANCES:** None
ELEVATION GAIN/LOSS: Minimal **DIFFICULTY:** Easy

Runners rave about the Barcelona Marathon because its route strikes a sweet spot that caters to elites and beginners alike. The terrain here is not only flat and fast, but it also passes at least 15 iconic sites thanks to a route revamp in 2024. Race officials describe the new course as "more urban, more central, and more monumental" than before, with a few portions doubling back to give runners and spectators a chance to see one another multiple times. To boot, the new route was designed to be fast—a course where runners have a chance to record best times.

Barcelona is known for its bold and varied architecture, heavily influenced by the work of Antoni Gaudí, a Catalan designer whose most recognizable work is probably the Basílica de la Sagrada Família, a towering, spindly Catholic church that runners pass just before kilometer 14. Although construction began on the building in 1882, it's not scheduled for completion until 2026, at which point it will be the world's tallest church.

Elsewhere on the route, runners get a glimpse of La Monumental, the arena used for bullfights, as well as Casa Batlló, another Gaudí design, with a facade decorated in a colorful mosaic of ceramic tiles (today, the house functions as an event space). Just before kilometer 10, participants cross the Bac de Roda Bridge, constructed for the 1992 Summer Olympics. This bridge links the districts of Sant Andreu (a more historic section of the city) and Sant Martí

WEATHER WATCH

March is one of the best times to visit Barcelona, with high temperatures topping out around 60°F (16°C). Take advantage of the thinner crowds this time of year, or start your trip early so you can pair the marathon with the tail end of Carnival, which sweeps across Spain from February to the early weeks of March.

Runners pass the Basílica de la Sagrada Família, Barcelona's famously unfinished church, near kilometer 14.

ABOVE: Tadesse Abraham of Switzerland celebrates his 2024 Barcelona Marathon victory.

OPPOSITE: The race's finish line is boisterous, with roaring crowds and confetti.

(known for Platja del Bogatell, a popular beach, as well as its lively music scene). At kilometer 16, take note of the Mercat del Ninot, a bustling shopping hub where you can load up on fresh fish, tapas, and delicious local wines after the race. Around the halfway point of the course, the route passes another market, Mercat de Sant Antoni.

Around kilometer 27, the urban landscape collides with refreshing views of the Mediterranean Sea for another two miles (3.2 km) before runners take a hard left back into the city. The landmark to aim toward now is the Torre Glòries, a skyscraper just beyond the 33-kilometer mark that is known as the gateway to Barcelona's tech district. Runners will turn around here and double back on the street they just traversed, so it's a good place for spectators to wait and cheer. The race's finish lies after a spectacular run through the Arc de Triomf, originally built in 1888 as the entrance to the World's Fair.

BERLIN MARATHON

The World Marathon Major for setting personal records

SEASON: Fall   **NO. OF MARATHON RUNNERS:** 48,000   **OTHER RACE DISTANCE:** 5K
ELEVATION GAIN/LOSS: 241 feet (73 m)/260 feet (79 m)   **DIFFICULTY:** Easy

There's a reason why so many of the world's best distance runners put the Berlin Marathon on their race schedule. It's a fast course, and the weather is typically between 55 and 70°F (13–21°C). In fact, the course is so fast that the men's and women's world records have been set there multiple times since the race's inception in 1974.

But you needn't be an elite athlete to run Berlin with lofty personal goals. The race is part of the series known as the World Marathon Majors, which includes the Tokyo, Boston, Chicago, New York City, and London Marathons. Of those six races, Berlin's claim to fame is its flat-as-a-pancake route with few turns, which makes it easy for runners to lock into and keep pace.

The Berlin Marathon celebrated its 50th anniversary in 2024 by paying homage to its unique history with an interactive exhibition that highlighted the race's ties to remarkable historic events, including the fall of the Berlin Wall and the overcoming of a political system. Nodding to the city's history, previous routes from the race weekend have passed by Olympic Stadium, built for the 1936 Games, where American sprinter Jesse Owens won four gold medals.

The marathon course features plenty of history hiding in plain sight. At the start of the race, runners will be close to the Reichstag's iconic glass dome—today, the building hosts Germany's national parliament, and you can

OPPOSITE: Kenya's Eliud Kipchoge waits at the starting line of the 2023 Berlin Marathon. He would go on to win the men's race for a record fifth time.

PAGES 102-103: The historic Brandenburg Gate marks the finish line.

still see scars on the facade from the damage it took in the Battle of Berlin during the Second World War. The course also takes the field through Alexanderplatz, one of the biggest commercial areas of the city, before the final stretch, which traverses Unter den Linden, the boulevard leading to the 18th-century Brandenburg Gate.

The finish is among the most historic on the marathon circuit, located just after runners pass through the Brandenburg Gate. This symbol of German unity can be an emotional passage for runners who remember the first time the course went through the gate in 1990, after the end of the Cold War and the fall of the Berlin Wall. That year, many participants stopped to kiss the ground before continuing to the finish.

One big perk at the finish line: massages for your tired legs. In fact, massage stations are available to runners every five kilometers beginning at kilometer 25. We can't say it makes for less achy legs the day after the race, but you'll certainly find it helpful for loosening tight muscles.

The festival that awaits on the grounds of the Reichstag includes showers and changing areas,

WHILE YOU'RE THERE

Extend your trip to Germany by stopping in Munich for Oktoberfest, which typically starts in September just a few days after the marathon. Oktoberfest is a celebration of Bavarian culture that includes carnival rides, games, and, of course, beer. It's about a two-hour flight from Berlin to Munich or a five-hour train ride.

a place to have a finisher medal engraved, standard refreshments, and non-alcoholic German beer. Want to imbibe? You're in Berlin. The city has countless beer-serving establishments.

If you're looking for a shakeout run or aren't quite ready to take on a full marathon, consider the Generali 5K the day before the marathon. It covers the last few miles of the marathon course and, like the main event, finishes at the Brandenburg Gate.

GETTING AROUND

Berlin has an excellent and efficient transit system. In recent years, race officials have sent an email to all participants with instructions to obtain a transit card. The card provides all runners with free access to the trains and metro from Thursday through Sunday of race weekend.

ABOVE: Ethiopia's Tigst Assefa won the 2023 Berlin Marathon women's race in record time: 2:11:53.

OPPOSITE: The Victory Column, commemorating the Prussian War, stands as motivation for every runner leaving the starting line.

BERMUDA MARATHON

A small race with a big crowd of local and enthusiastic supporters

SEASON: Winter **TOTAL NO. OF RUNNERS:** 1,300 **OTHER RACE DISTANCES:** 1 mile; 10K; half-marathon
ELEVATION GAIN/LOSS: 1,286 feet (392 m)/1,263 feet (385 m) **DIFFICULTY:** Moderate

Don't let the fear of getting lost in the fabled Bermuda Triangle stop you from signing up for this event. Visitors almost universally agree that the people of Bermuda are among the most warm, friendly, and welcoming anywhere. And that trademark hospitality is on full display during the Bermuda Triangle Challenge, which includes three races for those who dare to partake (you can also pick just one).

The weekend begins in downtown Hamilton, the capital of Bermuda, with a Friday road mile. The Royal Bermuda Regiment Band and Drum Corps plays to celebrate a race for local children from elementary to high school ages, as well as a thrilling elite race where professional runners go head-to-head in front of raucous spectators. On Saturday morning, the festivities continue with a 10K, which takes runners up to the highest point in Bermuda—260 feet (80 m) above sea level. But that's not to say that the area isn't hilly. It is. And on Sunday, marathon runners will find that out for themselves.

First, however, marathoners are ferried to the starting line on the west end of the island, at the Royal Naval Dockyard. The area is now a cruise ship port and major sightseeing, shopping, and dining attraction, but it once served as a base for Royal Marines during the War of 1812 and as a strategic British outpost during World War I and World War II. Early in the course, runners pass the Bermuda Railway Trail, which stretches from one end of the island to the

TRAINING TIP

The Bermuda Marathon is a small race, with only about 1,300 runners across all events. That means many participants will run alone for large portions of the course. Although the scenery might keep you company, try a few long solo training runs to get used to the solitude.

OPPOSITE: **There are few more beautiful—or aspirational—places to run 26.2 miles than Bermuda.**

PAGES 108-109: **Between sunny beaches and historic landmarks, Bermuda's lush tropical forests bring welcome shade to the course.**

other over 20 miles (32 km)—the marathon largely skirts this trail, and it's a nice place for a shakeout run. Then, participants tour some of the famous Bermuda beaches, including Horseshoe Bay, Jobson's Cove, and Warwick Long Bay, all known for the paradisial pink sand shores and clear blue water, as well as rocky inlets. The route continues into Flatts Village, the first official settlement on Bermuda, dating back to 1612. Today, Flatts Village is one of several quaint neighborhoods in an area noted for its pretty pastel-colored homes.

As the marathon continues along the island's north shore, runners drink in iconic views of the Atlantic Ocean. The scenery is timely, because by this point the undulating hills throughout the course might be taking their toll. And although mornings on Bermuda are usually cool, with an ocean breeze, the average daytime temperature is around 70°F (21°C), so make use of the on-course water stations. If you're already extra hydrated, keep in mind that the locals are known to offer rum to racers as well (but maybe save the traditional Bermudan Dark 'n' Stormy, a dark rum and ginger beer cocktail, for after the race).

GEAR CHECK

Although Bermuda has no rainy season, it has its fair share of showers from time to time. And some years the marathon has taken place in a downpour. Pack layers that will protect you from the elements, such as a waterproof running jacket and a hat with a visor to protect your face and eyes from rain or sun.

The race ends at Barr's Bay Park back in Hamilton. A party ensues with live music, free snacks and local beer, and those aforementioned rum cocktails. Before leaving the park, pay a visit to the "We Arrive" statue, which commemorates the 78 enslaved men, women, and children who arrived in Bermuda when the ship carrying them was blown off course in 1835. Slavery was outlawed in Bermuda, so the enslaved people aboard the *Enterprise* were released from bondage upon reaching the island.

If you're extending your visit to Bermuda beyond race day, Hamilton is a great place to stay. Home to the Hamilton Princess Resort and Beach Club (the iconic "Pink Palace," established in 1885) and Bacardi's new headquarters, the city boasts myriad restaurants, cafés, and shopping options on Front Street along Hamilton Harbour. You can also easily get to the iconic pink sand beaches by bus or cab from your Hamilton home base.

BOSTON MARATHON

A lifetime goal for runners across the globe

SEASON: **Spring** NO. OF MARATHON RUNNERS: **30,000** OTHER RACE DISTANCES: **Invitational Mile; 5K; 10K; half-marathon** ELEVATION GAIN/LOSS: **815 feet (248 m)/1,275 feet (389 m)** DIFFICULTY: **Moderate**

The Boston Marathon is the oldest annual marathon in the world, dating back to its first iteration in 1897. On the third Monday in April, the attention of all runners is on this New England tradition, held on what's known as Patriots' Day in Massachusetts. The holiday is unique to the region, originally held to recognize the Battles of Lexington and Concord, the first major military campaign of the American Revolution. Today, however, Patriots' Day serves as a celebration of the marathon and the Red Sox major league baseball team, who play at Boston's Fenway Park every year on the same date.

Runners must qualify for the Boston Marathon to gain entry, either by running a certified qualifying marathon within a specified time or by raising money for charity. The qualifying times have shifted over the years, and they vary based on age and gender. Running a Boston qualifier (known as a BQ) has become a crowning achievement for recreational runners around the world, to say nothing of running Boston itself!

Participants staying in Boston take a long school bus ride out to Hopkinton, 25 miles (40 km) west of the city, to the starting point of their journey back to Copley Square. The starting line is next to the Korean Presbyterian Church, where professional runners huddle while they wait for the race to begin. The first half of the course goes through the quintessential New England

RACE HISTORY

In 2013, the Boston Marathon was struck by tragedy when a bomb detonated near the finish line, killing three and injuring hundreds. Starting in 2015, the city began honoring the victims with One Boston Day every April 15. The city organizes community volunteering initiatives, acts of kindness, and remembrances.

OPPOSITE: The iconic Boston finish line is on Boylston Street, near Copley Square.

PAGES 114–115: The Boston field is competitive. Anyone who qualifies has the chance to run alongside the sport's top athletes.

hamlets of Ashland, Framingham, and Natick, where locals cheer on the field from their lawns.

Right before the halfway point of the race comes one of the long-standing traditions of the marathon: the Wellesley Scream Tunnel. You've never experienced a louder, more deafening stretch of road. The students and faculty at Wellesley College line up along campus to scream as loud as they can and display witty (sometimes irreverent) posters meant to inspire or make runners laugh. If you want to preserve your eardrums, veer to the left-hand side of the road—either way, it's a grand send-off into the most challenging part of the race: the Newton Hills. From miles 18 to 21, the net-downhill course presents its most significant uphill portion—the last and most notable of four ascents—known as Heartbreak Hill. It's about half a mile (0.8 km) to the top of the hill at a steep 3.5 percent gradient. But it's all downhill (almost) from there.

By mile 24, the crowds become dense as you near the city center, buoyed by Boston University students partying on both sides of

WHILE YOU'RE THERE

For a taste of local fare, have at least one lobster roll and a Samuel Adams 26.2 Brew—a Gose-style beer brewed with sea salt and coriander. If you're looking to warm up postrace, try the New England clam chowder to jump-start the refueling process.

ABOVE: **The entire city shuts down for Marathon Monday, aka Patriots' Day, and spectators celebrate by lining the streets to cheer on the field.**

OPPOSITE: **Up to 45 racers compete in the marathon's elite wheelchair divisions.**

Commonwealth Avenue and baseball fans gathering at Fenway. When you finally pass the giant Citgo sign on your left (the oil company installed the sign in 1940, and it has since become an unofficial landmark for marathoners), it's just a mile to go. Your quads might be on fire at this point from the descents, but keep going—the hardest parts are behind you. Take a right on Hereford Street, a left on Boylston Street, and soak in the last 600 meters. It's like running through a stadium with thousands of people cheering just for you. In addition to the onlookers, nearby Old South Church celebrates racers and volunteers by ringing the church bells (it's even dubbed itself the "Church of the Finish Line") in honor of one of the world's oldest races. Boston's finish line is one of the all-time greatest scenes in sports. And that is the magic of the Boston Marathon.

CALGARY MARATHON

A picturesque race through the foothills of the Canadian Rockies

SEASON: Spring   **NO. OF MARATHON RUNNERS:** 1,000   **OTHER RACE DISTANCES:** 5K; 10K; half-marathon; 60K (37.3 mi)
ELEVATION GAIN/LOSS: 437 feet (133 m)/437 feet (133 m)   **DIFFICULTY:** Easy

The Calgary Marathon experience can best be described as "communal." The race organization is known for its welcoming spirit, so much so that Rob Reid, a four-time winner, once said, "The Calgary Marathon takes hospitality to great heights, much like the scenic mountains nearby." Support extends to families with an on-site kids camp and four nursing stations (two on the course and one each at the start and finish) so child care isn't a barrier for parents' entry. Participants also enjoy crowd support for much of the race, which is always a buoy to any runner's spirit. It's all capped off with a finish-line party with food trucks, beer gardens, music, and massages.

Though the course has pockets of rolling hills that may feel challenging (even more so due to the out-and-back nature of the route), it offers fairly even terrain and an opportunity to clock your best time. Remember, though, that Calgary is some 3,430 feet (1,045 m) above sea level—enough altitude to make some flatlanders feel the difference. The best advice is to run by your effort level (70 percent effort, 80 percent effort, etc.), which might not always match your usual per-mile pace back at sea level.

The marathon begins and ends with western flair at Stampede Park, which is an event venue best known for the Calgary Stampede, the world's largest outdoor rodeo, held every July. Between, you'll see several city

OPPOSITE: A dedicated pace team makes the Calgary Marathon friendly to aspiring Boston qualifiers.

PAGES 120-121: Runners start near Stampede Park and the Scotiabank Saddledome.

neighborhoods, including artsy Inglewood at the confluence of the Elbow and Bow Rivers; Bridgeland, home to the Calgary Zoo; and Kensington, known to be the city's center for dining and entertainment (note Kensington as a place you can return to for celebrating and nourishment after your run).

Runners turn around at kilometer 26 (around mile 16) to head back the way they came. Beware: The last five miles (8 km) or so can turn hot. Running along the Bow River Pathway offers little shade, and the average high temperature is 70°F (21°C). Nonetheless, the pathway is a nice place for a shakeout run. Or, if you're looking to get out of the urbanscape, head to Nose Hill Park in the northwest quadrant of Calgary to hit some trails and take in beautiful views of the city and mountains.

APRÈS RACE

You'd be remiss to visit Alberta without a stop at Banff National Park, about 90 minutes west of Calgary. The Canadian Rockies, turquoise glacial lakes, and endless trails are breathtaking. Don't miss canoeing on Lake Louise, where you'll find yourself on emerald water and surrounded by majestic mountain peaks.

CAYMAN ISLANDS MARATHON

A perfectly flat course along a major cruising port

SEASON: Winter   **NO. OF MARATHON RUNNERS: 200**   **OTHER RACE DISTANCES: Half-marathon; 4-person marathon relay**   **ELEVATION GAIN/LOSS: Minimal**   **DIFFICULTY: Easy**

The marathon starts in the predawn hours to avoid the hottest part of the day, though you're in the Caribbean, so you'll likely still feel hot by the finish with temperatures averaging 85°F (29°C). But the early wake-up call offers more than just beating the heat: Runners can relish the opportunity to watch the sun rise halfway through the race. The moment of peace and tranquility while running by the ocean at daybreak is reason enough to sign up for the Cayman Islands Marathon.

The event takes place in George Town, the capital of the Cayman Islands and a major port for Caribbean cruise ships. The white sand beaches and the opportunity to snorkel or scuba dive near the coral reef are big draws. The race itself is two loops of the same course (brace yourself for passing the finish line when you still have a half-marathon to go!), and you'll begin each loop by trekking through the financial district of George Town before you reach the South Sound, where you'll take in ocean views.

There's no better way to recover from a marathon than jumping into the ocean and relaxing on the beach with coconut water or a Caybrew beer. Consider booking accommodations on Seven Mile Beach, known as one of the world's best shores, and replenish your stores with island cuisine, including jerk chicken and "rundown," a stew of coconut milk and pimiento peppers with onions, potatoes, and beef or seafood.

Oddy Grullon of the Dominican Republic was the first female runner to finish the 2023 Cayman Islands Marathon.

CHICAGO MARATHON

A fast, favorite course in a fun city

SEASON: **Fall**   NO. OF MARATHON RUNNERS: **50,000**   OTHER RACE DISTANCE: **5K**
ELEVATION GAIN/LOSS: **243 feet (74 m)/242 feet (74 m)**   DIFFICULTY: **Easy**

For a big-city marathon, Chicago makes the logistics easier than most. Hotels within walking distance of the start and finish in Grant Park are plentiful, and taking the Chicago Transit Authority rail and bus system is a cinch. The course itself is a grand tour of one of the most beloved U.S. cities, and spectators can spot their participant up to four times by walking only about a mile within the looped route.

This is a golden opportunity for those who like to keep a metronomic pace. Set it and forget it—almost the entire route is flat, except for one sneaky little incline within 400 meters of the finish line. The men's and women's marathon world records have been set in Chicago multiple times, which is always an indication that fast times are possible for everybody in the field. The conditions are often favorable, with an average high of 62°F (17°C), though the race weekend has experienced unusually hot weather several times in recent years. Like with any race, runners should prepare for anything Mother Nature has in store. And though Chicago may be dubbed the Windy City, gusts are often not a factor in the race—the course largely steers clear of Lake Michigan's shoreline, where the breeze is most noticeable.

Grant Park's 319 acres (129 ha) serve as the staging area for the race, as well as the starting and finish line. The park is flanked on the east side by Lake Michigan, and its centerpiece is the Buckingham Fountain, one of the largest

OPPOSITE: **Chicago runners head north from the starting line, within a shoe's throw of Lake Michigan.**

PAGES 126-127: **Runners cross five downtown bridges throughout the course.**

fountains in the world. Here you can also find the "Cloud Gate" sculpture, more commonly known as "The Bean."

After the start, the course winds its way through 29 different Chicago neighborhoods. Some of the highlights include Lincoln Park, where supporters catch athletes running by the Lincoln Park Zoo at mile six and again at mile 10. The crowds are especially boisterous in Wrigleyville, home of Major League Baseball's Chicago Cubs and their stadium, Wrigley Field, though truth be told, the entire race route is well attended, offering a vivid display of the city's diversity and energy.

The route takes a turn through Chinatown at mile 22, where traditional Chinese music and dragon dancers greet runners, and passes through the Chinatown gate, which is painted red to symbolize good luck. At a pivotal moment late in the race, the gate brings a welcome boost of cheer and energy.

Pace teams are a big part of the Chicago Marathon (in fact, I've served on one myself!). Pacers

WHAT TO EAT

Three major chains fight for supremacy in the Chicago deep-dish pizza scene: Gino's East, Lou Malnati's, and Giordano's. Locals have their preferences, but visitors won't miss out no matter where they go. However, if you plan ahead or sit out a long wait, Pequod's in Lincoln Park offers a caramelized deep-dish pizza that by itself might justify a visit to the Windy City.

hold signs with the group's goal time the entire way, from start to finish. If you have a particular goal in mind, all you have to do is find the pacer assigned to that goal and follow the leader. Just be sure to mind how you're feeling. There's no shame in hitting a speed boost to beat your predetermined pace, or easing up to join runners in a later group. The Chicago streets are a perfect place to put your training to the test.

ABOVE: Kenya's Kelvin Kiptum crossed the 2023 finish line in 2:00:35, a new world record.

OPPOSITE: As many as 50,000 runners take off from the starting line in Grant Park.

WHERE TO STAY

Grant Park has a plethora of hotels within a walking radius of the start and finish lines, so there's no need to worry about transportation on race morning. If you stay in the downtown Loop, you'll find yourself near popular tourist destinations like Navy Pier, the Magnificent Mile, and the pedestrian pathway along Lake Michigan.

WALT DISNEY WORLD MARATHON

The most magical 26.2 miles on Earth

SEASON: Winter   **NO. OF MARATHON RUNNERS: 13,000**   **OTHER RACE DISTANCES: 5K; 10K; half-marathon; Goofy's Race and a Half Challenge; Dopey Challenge**   **ELEVATION GAIN/LOSS: 351 feet (107 m)/354 feet (108 m)**   **DIFFICULTY: Easy**

Running through (and around) all four of Walt Disney World's theme parks—EPCOT, Magic Kingdom, Animal Kingdom Theme Park, and Disney's Hollywood Studios—is a dream for many of the company's biggest fans. Getting cheers from celebrities like Mickey Mouse and Donald Duck? Beyond wildest imaginations. Combining two passions into a four-day (or more) vacation? As the hosts themselves say: "Every mile is magic."

The Walt Disney World Marathon is part of a weekend like no other, which begins on Thursday morning with a 5K, followed by a Friday 10K, a half-marathon on Saturday, and the marathon on Sunday. While participants can choose which events they want to do, many go for both the half- and full marathons to complete Goofy's Race and a Half Challenge. Finishing all four races earns you the Dopey Challenge—plus six T-shirts and six finisher medals (one for each race, plus one for each challenge).

The marathon begins at 5 a.m. in EPCOT's parking lot, in the shadow of the landmark sphere known as Spaceship Earth. Make sure to plan out your running-friendly costume—many runners dress up as their favorite Disney characters (lots of tiaras, tutus, and mouse ears). A firework send-off starts things for each group of the race. Many of the miles on the course traverse highways and roads that connect the Walt Disney World properties, though runners always have a new theme park to look forward to. Of course, one

WHERE TO STAY

The easiest way to navigate race logistics is to stay at a Disney resort, where shuttle buses are provided to take you everywhere you need to be—including the runDisney Health & Fitness Expo, which is held at the ESPN Wide World of Sports Complex.

OPPOSITE: Confetti showers the podium finishers for each event on race weekend. Sometimes, it greets the caboose as well.

PAGES 132-133: Each wave gets its own fireworks send-off as runners begin the Walt Disney World Marathon.

of the most iconic stops along the course for Disney fans is Magic Kingdom. It's a rare chance to run up Main Street U.S.A. (where your family and friends are welcome to watch), through Tomorrowland (to infinity and beyond!), and through Cinderella Castle. In Animal Kingdom Theme Park, runners make their way past the towering peak of the Expedition Everest roller coaster. At Disney's Hollywood Studios, don't be frightened by screams coming from the beloved Tower of Terror as you pass by. The marathon also includes a lakefront jaunt in EPCOT around its World Showcase, the 11 pavilions exhibiting different countries and cuisines.

The cast of characters who station themselves along the course changes each year, but runners can expect to see the mainstays such as Mickey and Minnie. Other characters cheering on marathoners may include Chip and Dale, Daisy Duck, and Cruella de Vil. Go ahead and wave to Winnie the Pooh and friends, or Belle. Participants are encouraged to stop and have pictures taken along the way.

APRÈS RACE

Though most visitors to Orlando stick close to Walt Disney World, the city offers other attractions too. Downtown Orlando is about a 30-minute drive from Walt Disney World. Take a stroll or a shakeout run around Lake Eola, where you'll find local restaurants, a night market on weekends, and live music at the amphitheater. This is an up-and-coming running city. The 2024 Olympic marathon trials were held here.

DUBLIN MARATHON

The "friendly marathon"

SEASON: Fall NO. OF MARATHON RUNNERS: **20,000** OTHER RACE DISTANCES: **None**
ELEVATION GAIN/LOSS: **682 feet (208 m)/703 feet (214 m)** DIFFICULTY: **Easy**

Since its inaugural running in 1980, the Dublin Marathon has started and ended near Merrion Square in the city center. As the race has grown, the local government and transit officials have considered relocating the race to an area where street closures would inconvenience fewer residents and visitors, but organizers (as well as runners) have resisted that change.

The event typically starts on Fitzwilliam Street and ends in one of Dublin's largest Georgian squares, where you'll see the homes of historical figures and celebrities who once lived there, like famous Irish poet W. B. Yeats and Daniel O'Connell, aka "the Liberator," the leader of Ireland's Roman Catholic majority in the early 19th century.

Beware: You'll need a little luck to secure a spot on the starting line—it sells out quickly even though it convenes one of the largest marathon fields in Europe. Registration is held as a lottery, and runners don't need to have qualifying times to participate. If you don't secure a spot, keep an eye out: If people drop out, their spots are offered on a first-come, first-served basis on the race's website.

Weather for the race is ideal for runners. The average temperature around race weekend is in the mid-50s Fahrenheit (around 13°C), and Dublin belies Ireland's reputation for rainfall, so getting wet isn't really a worry.

The course is mostly flat, with a few rolling hills to contend with, especially late in the race at Ireland's "Heartbreak Hill"—a long, gradual incline on

OPPOSITE: **Dublin's famed Ha'penny Bridge often graces the marathon's finisher medal.**

PAGES 136-137: **A race through Dublin's city center means lots of cheering locals.**

Roebuck Road that starts around mile 22. The big loop around Ireland's capital city also showcases its history, parks, and unique neighborhoods, as well as Irish culture. The cutoff finishing time is seven hours, which is friendly to a wide range of marathoners. The people in Dublin—runners and spectators alike—are amiable, enthusiastic, and passionate about the rich tradition of distance running.

Within the first mile, marathoners pass St. Stephen's Green Park, notable for the 1916 Easter Rising, when the Irish Citizen Army staged an armed insurrection (though they temporarily ceased gunfire while the park's groundskeeper fed the ducks). In the following early miles, the route passes Christ Church Cathedral, established in 1030. The cathedral's famous bells date to 1738.

After traversing James Joyce Bridge over the River Liffey, marathoners head to Phoenix Park, one of the largest urban parks in Europe and home to the Dublin Zoo, where a large herd of fallow deer roam (the zoo is great for shakeout

TRAVEL TIP

As with many of the bigger international marathons, going to the race with a tour company can take a load of logistical planning (travel, accommodations, meals, ground transportation, etc.) off your plate. Many of these companies have official affiliations with the race organizations, so check the race website to find one that meets your needs. See if they also host excursions to explore all Dublin has to offer outside of the marathon.

ABOVE: Irish Olympian Noel Carroll (center, white T-shirt) participates in the inaugural Dublin Marathon in 1980. Carroll helped found the race.

OPPOSITE: The course makes its way through Dublin's Phoenix Park for miles 3 through 10.

runs and postrace walks too). Around mile 10 comes the first significant hill, called the St. Laurence Road Hill. This stretch to the halfway point is loaded with boisterous spectators that help motivate. Between miles 17 and 18, participants go through Bushy Park, where the Allied forces of the Second World War planned Operation Overlord, better known as the D-Day landings in Normandy.

Then it's on to the aforementioned Heartbreak Hill (named after the Boston Marathon's famous incline, see page 112). Dublin's Heartbreak is located in picturesque Orwell Park, near University College Dublin, Ireland's largest university. Take a deep breath—the hills are over after this one. Now you can enjoy a fast dash back to Merrion Square, where the finish line awaits. In a matter of time, you'll be kicking back at a local pub or touring the famous Guinness Storehouse, which offers a range of tours and tastings.

GREAT WALL MARATHON

Temperatures and terrain make this marathon among the most challenging in the world.

SEASON: Spring   **NO. OF MARATHON RUNNERS: 2,500**   **OTHER RACE DISTANCES: 8.5K (5.3 mi); half-marathon**
ELEVATION GAIN/LOSS: 2,493 feet (760 m)/2,493 feet (760 m)   **DIFFICULTY: Challenging**

This race brings new meaning to the phrase "hitting the wall," that's for sure. The Great Wall Marathon offers by far one of the most unique settings for a run—and requires a significant amount of preparation to finish. But running the Great Wall Marathon is also an experience—and a challenge—of a lifetime. One for the history books, some might say.

To register for the race, international participants must book a six- or seven-day tour package through the race organization. Guests stay either in Jizhou, near the race venue of Huangyaguan, or in the capital city of Beijing, which is a bit more than an hour's drive to the starting line (transportation is included).

The marathon starts and ends in Yin and Yang Square and incorporates the section of the Great Wall in Tianjin Province. The Great Wall was constructed as a west-to-east barrier to defend northern China from enemy attacks. Its full historical extent is around 21,196 kilometers (13,171 mi), beginning at Jiayuguan Pass in the west and ending at the Bohai Sea.

Participants in the race first run on surrounding highways and roads to reach the wall's entrance—a four-kilometer (2.5 mi) hill leads to the first of the 5,164 steps you'll climb throughout the race. Around kilometer seven, you'll meet a steep descent on the Goat Track, a single-track section that includes

WHILE YOU'RE THERE

Your tour usually offers options for excursions, including to the Forbidden City, a palace complex that dates back to the Ming and Qing dynasties, and the Temple of Heaven, founded in the 15th century.

OPPOSITE: No shame in using your hands to make your way up a few of the marathon's 5,164 steps.

PAGES 142-143: Try not to strain yourself during the starting-line hype.

a handrail for safety. Take note—you'll come back up this section toward the end of the race. After passing through Yin and Yang Square again, the marathon follows the Yellow River to Duanzhuang village and on toward the township of Xiaying. This stage is a chance to appreciate China's rural landscape and farmlands before eventually getting to Chedaoyu village, where another steep incline awaits. You'll go past the finish line yet again before heading back to the Great Wall for a second time, via the Goat Track (going up this time). Take in the stunning views of the rugged mountains surrounding the wall before you enjoy the relief of the downhill finish.

At some points on the Great Wall, the stairs are so steep that runners climb on all fours to get to the top. These steps vary in height and width, and some are made of brick and others are uneven stone, so footing can be tricky. And sometimes there are no steps at all, just rocks and concrete. One thing is constant: Runners must pay attention to what they're doing as they navigate so many different types of terrain. The race provides aid stations and hydration every four kilometers (2.5 mi), but runners should consider having their own hydration handy. On average, the temperature is around 77°F (25°C), but it can be much warmer, up to 95°F (35°C), with high humidity.

HANOI HERITAGE MARATHON

A historic tour through the Vietnamese capital

SEASON: Fall   **NO. OF MARATHON RUNNERS: 11,000**   **OTHER RACE DISTANCES: 5K; 10K; half-marathon**
ELEVATION GAIN/LOSS: Minimal   **DIFFICULTY: Moderate**

The Hanoi Heritage Marathon is a looped course that navigates through more than a thousand years of history, representing what the organizers describe as the "peaceful country and amicable people of Vietnam." The name Hanoi translates to "city of lakes," so it's fitting that the marathon begins and ends at Hoan Kiem Lake, the historical center of the city. Along the route, runners pass several significant landmarks, including the Temple of Literature, dedicated to Confucius, and the Ho Chi Minh Mausoleum, the resting place of the revolutionary leader. The course ends after the O Quan Chuong, the ancient city's gate in the middle of Hanoi, which once served as a security checkpoint for the Old Quarter.

While the route itself is scenic (though not especially challenging), the weather can add an element of difficulty. The average high temperature is 66°F (19°C), but the humidity can hover at 84 percent.

Hanoi is a fascinating place to visit, and its cuisine is delectable. Ever since former president Barack Obama and famed chef and television personality Anthony Bourdain ate at Bun Cha Huong Lien on an episode of *Parts Unknown*, tourists have flocked to the no-frills eatery. Today it serves the "Combo Obama"—*bun cha* (a traditional dish of pork and noodles), a crab spring roll, and a bottle of Hanoi Beer, which will set you back about $3.50. What better way to fuel up for 26.2 miles?

The marathon takes you along the lush boundaries of the Red River.

HELSINKI CITY MARATHON

Run a few loops through the capital city's greatest hits.

SEASON: Summer   **NO. OF MARATHON RUNNERS:** 1,000   **OTHER RACE DISTANCES:** 10K; half-marathon; marathon relay   **ELEVATION GAIN/LOSS:** Minimal   **DIFFICULTY:** Easy

Late August in Helsinki could very well be rainy, but you'll still enjoy more than 14 hours of daylight—enough to explore the capital of Finland to the fullest. From Nordic minimalist architecture to art nouveau, Helsinki is a treat for design aficionados or anybody who appreciates unique cityscapes. The city's marathon course—which begins and ends in Meripuisto, a gorgeous seaside park overlooking the Gulf of Finland—makes a great tour in and of itself.

The marathon has a large opening loop that takes runners through a few popular neighborhoods of Helsinki, as well as along the shorelines of the gulf. Among the first areas the course includes is Hietalahti, home to an eponymous shipyard. You'll also pass by the Luonnontieteellinen Museo, or Natural History Museum, on a short out-and-back stretch through the city center. Soon the route swings around the West Harbour in the Jätkäsaari district. This is another opportunity to gaze at the sea before heading back toward the finish area, which is where you started. You'll cover a smaller loop in the area surrounding Meripuisto two more times before crossing the finish line. For those who like to get into a rhythm and revisit the same sites several times as distance markers, this is the course for you.

Finland has a rich history in distance running, and visitors to Helsinki can check out many neighborhoods on foot. Though the race course largely

APRÈS RACE

Pay homage to the Flying Finn Paavo Nurmi, the legendary Finnish middle-distance runner who set 20 world records and won nine Olympic gold medals in the 1920s. A statue of Nurmi sits outside of Olympic Stadium in Helsinki, the site of the 1952 Summer Games.

From the starting line, you'll head south into the residential Töölö neighborhood for the first kilometer.

avoids the city center, it's walkable or accessible by public transit—and it's perfect for a shakeout run or walking tour after the marathon. Don't miss Central Park, which extends about 6 miles (10 km) from the city center in Laakso to the Vantaa River. The park is a Finnish forest oasis for urban dwellers, with gravel trails, meadows, and spaces for outdoor recreation. If the waterfront is more your scene, head to Lauttasaari, an island west of the city, which you can access by Metro. The entire way around the island is also about 6 miles (10 km).

A sauna is the perfect indulgence for any recovering marathoner. Löyly, situated on the Baltic Sea, is one of the most well known in Finland. Refuel at the accompanying restaurant, which serves classic regional fare, such as meatballs and creamy salmon soup.

ABOVE: **The Finnish flag waves over the Gulf of Finland.**

OPPOSITE: **The finish line is at Helsinki Olympic Stadium, host of the 1952 Summer Olympics.**

HONOLULU MARATHON

It's all "aloha" along this course that races its way through a tropical paradise.

SEASON: Winter   **NO. OF MARATHON RUNNERS:** 14,000   **OTHER RACE DISTANCES:** 1 mile; 10K
ELEVATION GAIN/LOSS: 457 feet (139 m)/455 feet (138 m)   **DIFFICULTY:** Moderate

Picture this: It's early December and you're about to start a marathon on a street called Ala Moana Boulevard, Hawaiian for "path by the ocean." What better version of paradise can there be? The Honolulu Marathon course is largely an out-and-back setup that doesn't stray far from near-constant views of the Pacific surf.

Given the extreme sea level location, you'd think that the route would remain relatively flat. But a long climb from mile eight to mile nine on the course tops out at Diamond Head, an extinct volcanic crater with sweeping views over Honolulu. This is the highest point on the course, and you'll encounter it twice—once out, and once on the way back at mile 24. It's mostly downhill to the finish from there.

You have quite a bit of territory to cover on the island of Oahu. First you'll traverse some urban terrain through Waikiki's high-rise hotels before you're treated to a lovely view of Waikiki Beach and its famous white sand. After the sun comes up—the race starts at 5 a.m. to avoid the heat of the day, which can reach into the 80s Fahrenheit (27–32°C) with tropical humidity—you won't be able to get enough of the coastline vistas. After mile 10, participants log about four miles (6.4 km) on the Kalanianaole Highway, which can get hot because it's exposed. If you're looking for a retreat from the heat, take a gander at the gorgeous luxury homes built into the cliffs. There's nothing

RACE WEEKEND TIP

Don't miss the Kalakaua Merrie Mile on Saturday. The one-mile race along the street next to Waikiki Beach includes some of the fastest professional runners in the world and is a good chance to double your race bling! Afterward, grab your postrace food and drinks in the festival area on the beach.

OPPOSITE: The Waikiki skyline includes Kapi'olani Regional Park, Kuhio Beach, and Diamond Head.

PAGES 152–153: Hydration packs can be worth the weight as the sun rises on the course.

like some dreamy island real estate to motivate your miles.

Shortly after mile 16, runners start to turn back, covering much of the same route as they did heading out. Near the turn, look for Koko Head, another volcanic crater, this one by Hanauma Bay (a popular place to snorkel after the marathon!). The finish is at Kapi'olani Regional Park, home to the Honolulu Zoo. (Pro tip: If you're driving, park here before the race and take a complimentary shuttle to the starting line.) Unlike most big-city races, the Honolulu Marathon doesn't have a cut-off time, so the finish area remains open until the last person crosses the line (it's not unusual for the caboose of the race to arrive after around 17 hours). It's called the "aloha spirit" or the "coordination of mind and heart within each person." The hearts of Hawaiian people are rooted in warmth, affection, and kindness for the good of the whole. The final finishers often report how enthusiastic crowds and other runners cheered them on through their final miles.

Don't leave the park without picking up your free freshly made *malasada,* a doughnut-like pastry first brought to Hawaii by Portuguese laborers who worked on the sugar plantations.

ISTANBUL MARATHON

An intercontinental event that stretches from Asia to Europe

SEASON: Fall **TOTAL NO. OF RUNNERS:** 45,000 **OTHER RACE DISTANCE:** 15K
ELEVATION GAIN/LOSS: 1,128 feet (344 m)/1,166 feet (355 m) **DIFFICULTY:** Moderate

The Istanbul Marathon traverses two continents. The race begins with a 1,560-meter jaunt (about a mile) across the 15 July Martyrs Bridge, which spans the Bosporus, the waterway that cuts through the city and divides Europe and Asia. The views of the strait from this vantage point are stunning, with the Istanbul skyline ahead. The route continues on to pass many significant historical sites, including Dolmabahçe Palace, a relic of the Ottoman Empire with 285 rooms and 46 halls, and Topkapı Palace, which once served as the administrative headquarters and residence of the imperial Ottoman court. Another highlight is the Sultan Ahmet Mosque, or Blue Mosque, where the finish line awaits. This majestic structure was built in 1609 and is still a popular place of worship today.

Running through some of the oldest settlements in the world is a treasured experience. Istanbul embraces Western and Eastern cultures, giving visitors a taste of both in a stunning location. Turkey offers its own culinary delights to feast upon before and after the race—chief among them is *knafeh,* a spun pastry soaked in a sugary syrup called attar and layered with clotted cream, pistachios, or cheese.

To get the most out of your visit, book a hotel near the finish line, which is close to many of the city's most popular attractions. Show your race bib for free public transportation to the starting line.

The Galata Tower on Istanbul's European side provides a monumental backdrop for runners.

KAUAI, HAWAII, U.S.A.

KAUAI MARATHON

A marathon made for those who can't get enough exercise

SEASON: Fall **TOTAL NO. OF RUNNERS:** 1,800 **OTHER RACE DISTANCE:** Half-marathon
ELEVATION GAIN/LOSS: 2,171 feet (662 m)/2,182 feet (665 m) **DIFFICULTY:** Challenging

The Kauai Marathon takes place along the stunning southern coast of the northernmost island of Hawaii. The fusion of a gorgeous setting with a celebration of local culture makes this race special—and it is growing in popularity: In 2023, race organizers reported that the island sold out of rental cars and hotel rooms on the south side of the island for race weekend.

The race begins in the predawn hours near Poipu Beach, a popular resort destination. Like at many distance-running events held in warm climates, the typical early wake-up call for this race is worth it to avoid the hottest part of the day—temperatures can reach into the 80s Fahrenheit (27–29°C) with the typical high humidity you'd expect in Hawaii. Before sunrise, tiki torches light the way and the sound of conch shells signifies the official start. The first mile (1.6 km) is flat, but don't get comfortable—it doesn't stay that way for long. The next six miles (9.7 km) are a gradual climb that culminates in the Tunnel of Trees, a mile-long stretch beneath a shady canopy of eucalyptus trees planted more than 100 years ago. Though the incline is long and difficult, you'll find three aid stations along the way, as well as local hula dancers—including the award-winning group Hālau Ka Lei Mokihana o Leinā'ala—there to buoy your spirits. Take heart: After passing the Tunnel of Trees, you've completed the hardest part of the race.

TRAVEL TIP

While you're in Kauai, tour the iconic Nā Pali coast. If you want to hike the Kalalau Trail, a 22-mile (35.4 km) round trip from Ke'e Beach to Kalalau Beach, you'll need to get a permit (see *KalalauTrail.com*). The tired feet may be worth the effort to see the waterfall made famous by *Jurassic Park*.

OPPOSITE: Long coastal roads offer competitors fantastic beach views.

PAGES 158-159: The finish line is one turn off Hoai Bay—consider soaking your feet in the Pacific after you're done.

As you descend into the Omao neighborhood, look inland for rainbows—it's often raining over the mountains, which leads to some gorgeous scenery. Then, marathoners (called "big chickens" as a nod to the thousands of feral chickens that roam throughout the island) diverge from half-marathoners ("little chickens") to complete a loop in Kalaheo, where the Kauai Coffee Company grows and roasts its famous beans (come back later to tour the plantation). Enjoy the ocean vista in the distance as well as the downhill miles to the finish. Many of the residents wait on their lawns to spray down runners with hoses or hand out drinks and candy. The race ends with another oceanfront view at Koloa Landing, a resort haven on Poipu Beach. Native Hawaiians greet runners by placing finisher medals around their necks, in much the same way that local hotels greet you with a floral lei at check-in.

Beyond the finish line, a party awaits where the island spirit and community come alive. Top finishers in both the marathon and half-marathon receive locally crafted awards, including hand-painted plates. Local entertainers such as *taiko*

APRÈS RACE

Put Waimea Canyon, on the west side of the island, on your must-see list. It's the "Grand Canyon of the Pacific," extending 3,600 feet (1,100 m) deep and 14 miles (22.5 km) long. Take Waimea Canyon Drive to Koke'e State Park if you're looking for more trails to explore, or to shake out your legs before or after the marathon.

drummers entertain runners and their families and friends. Cold beer, rice fig bars, Hawaiian chips, chicken and veggie wraps, and iced coffee drinks are served until the afternoon hours.

A trip to Poipu Beach, named "America's Best Beach" by the Travel Channel, at sunset is a wonderful way to wind down after a long race day. It's a great spot to watch sea turtles come ashore (keep a safe and respectful distance). Monk seals are another popular local species. They prefer to sunbathe on the sand, so be sure to stay back at least 100 feet (30 m) from their resting places. If you're still famished from your run efforts, make a stop at Puka Dog, which serves up a uniquely Hawaiian hot dog (think freshly toasted buns, tropical relishes, and passion fruit mustard) as well as Hawaiian shave ice. If you're not too tired the next morning, you can wake up early to watch the sea turtles return to the ocean back on Poipu Beach.

LISBON MARATHON

A coastal race rivaling Big Sur for spectacle

SEASON: Fall **NO. OF MARATHON RUNNERS: 5,000** **OTHER RACE DISTANCES: 8K (5 mi); half-marathon**
ELEVATION GAIN/LOSS: Minimal **DIFFICULTY: Easy**

Although Lisbon is known for its hills, the city's marathon sticks to the Atlantic coastline for a mostly flat course that prioritizes epic ocean views over grueling climbs. The route begins in Cascais, a historic summertime retreat west of Lisbon. Most runners take a 40-minute train ride from Lisbon to Cascais on race day, where the race course itself leads them back toward Lisbon to Praça do Comércio, one of the capital's most breathtaking and palatial squares overlooking the Tagus River.

Though the point-to-point course has stretches without spectators, and portions far from the city center, the sound of the waves crashing against Portugal's many beaches as you run along the coastline offers a serene, if not downright relaxing, soundtrack to quieter parts of the route. The crowds become more plentiful the closer you get to the city.

The first landmark of the course is the red lighthouse in Cabo Raso, around kilometer seven. This is the westernmost point of mainland Europe. Once you're past the lighthouse, cliffside luxury homes compete with the ocean for your attention until—at almost the halfway point—the course hits a few popular surfing beaches. Though the choicest waves might not arrive until winter, there will still be plenty of morning action to watch. Keep your eyes peeled for a "barrel"—when a surfer rides inside a wave tube.

The route turns onto a red promenade along the beach, winding around

APRÈS RACE

Lisbon's steep hills can offer an unwelcome obstacle to exhausted runners in the days following the marathon. If you want to avoid hiking the inclines, take Tram 28, a historic train that runs past most of the city's major tourist destinations.

OPPOSITE: The Castelo de São Jorge, or Saint George's Castle, rises above the Lisbon skyline.

PAGES 164–165: The course passes through Lisbon's Baixa district, an excellent place for shopping and dining before or after the race.

the Fort of Santo Amaro do Areeiro, originally constructed in the mid-1600s to protect the city and estuary during the Portuguese Restoration War. This can be a tranquil point in the marathon to take in the water and appreciate the even, sea-level terrain, but beware: This portion has no shade to protect you from the sun, and the heat could sneak up on you if it's a warm day (high temperatures in fall average 75°F [24°C]). A hat and sunglasses are highly advised. Around the 30-kilometer mark, you'll start to see Lisbon ahead as you approach the final beach on the course. Look for the Fort of São Bruno here, built in the 1600s and one of the course's most historic landmarks.

Belém Tower is your indication that you've made it back to Lisbon. Fittingly, this fortification was built in the 1500s as the ceremonial gateway to the city for explorers. The crowd support is louder at this point—and most participants find they need it after so much sun and heat—as the course follows a promenade and through the Rua Augusta Arch to the finish line. The final stretch also features cobblestone streets, which can be an added challenge for runners with feet or ankle

TRAVEL TIP

Don't miss a fado music experience, also known as the "Lisbon blues." Fado is a genre that centers mostly on ballads about heartbreak, usually accompanied by a mandolin or another stringed instrument. You can find fado bars in the Alfama or Bairro Alto neighborhoods.

trouble. Consider high-cushion shoes, or even extra ankle support if you're known to have a hard time with uneven terrain (especially at the end of a long run).

The final challenges of the course pair with Lisbon's ancient, eclectic architecture. The colors in Europe's second oldest city (it's 400 years older than Rome) are dazzling, and the blend of history and culture is second to none.

After you cross the finish line and celebrate, treat yourself to a *pastel de nata*, perhaps Portugal's most famous dessert. This egg custard pastry is a featured item at most local patisseries—you can try it plain or sprinkled with cinnamon. You may also want to cap your celebration with a taste of *ginjinha*, a Portuguese cherry liqueur meant for sipping. You can find pastel de nata throughout Lisbon, but some of the best is served at Manteigaria, which has eight bakeries across the city.

ABOVE: Lisbon's Tagus Estuary Natural Reserve leads out to the Atlantic Ocean.

OPPOSITE: The Rua Augusta Arch overlooks the finish line.

LEWA SAFARI MARATHON

Run wild on a marathon course designed to preserve its surroundings.

SEASON: Southern Hemisphere fall   **NO. OF MARATHON RUNNERS:** 300   **OTHER RACE DISTANCES:** 5K; 10K; half-marathon   **ELEVATION GAIN/LOSS:** 1,427 feet (435 m)/1,427 feet (435 m)   **DIFFICULTY:** Challenging

I t's called "The World's Wildest Challenge" for good reason. The Lewa Safari Marathon is held in Kenya's Lewa Wildlife Conservancy, home to Africa's legendary big five: lions, elephants, rhinoceroses, leopards, and African buffalo. You may also spot cheetahs, zebras, hyenas, and wild dogs along the way—if you're lucky. Don't panic: The route has plenty of security—armed rangers patrol the course, and two helicopters and one spotter plane fly above, looking for danger. Most animals tend to steer clear of crowds like the one that gathers on race day, but some seem undeterred by the festivities. In a recent race, a helicopter had to hover over a rhinoceros and encourage it off the course as runners approached.

Rhino encounters aside, the high altitude is actually your biggest risk factor: The course sits at 5,500 feet (1,680 m) above sea level. Weather is another risk. Marathoners run on dirt roads around the conservancy grounds in about 90°F (32°C) heat. You're not likely to smash a personal record at the Lewa Safari Marathon, but you will compete for a great cause and have a fantastic experience. To enter the race, all participants agree to a minimum fundraising commitment with all proceeds supporting wildlife preservation and anti-poaching programs, as well as schools and health care initiatives across Kenya. In fact, race organizers have taken international participants to visit some of the schools that have benefited from their fundraising

WHERE TO STAY

Staying at the camp set up for the race adds to the camaraderie of participation. The camp becomes its own athlete village, with walk-in tents equipped with twin or double beds. Each tent has its own bathroom (a short drop toilet) and hot-water bucket shower. The common area includes a bar and mess tent. Three meals are included each day.

For some, a zebra sighting might be as coveted as a finisher medal.

ABOVE: **Three Masai giraffes graze in the Lewa Wildlife Conservancy.**

OPPOSITE: **At this marathon, Kenya celebrates both its wildlife and a long tradition of championship distance running.**

efforts, allowing them to see the impact of their donations and to build a sense of community and purpose with the event. Across the race's 25-plus-year history, funds raised by marathoners have exceeded $4 million.

On race day, runners cover two loops over rolling hills, where they traverse savanna plains marked by scattered trees and tall grass. The route takes participants along riverbanks and through acacia woodlands, known for their bright yellow flowers.

The race start can be chaotic and dusty with so many people aiming for a narrow dirt road, but with the field of half-marathoners and marathoners capped at 1,200 people, it quickly thins out. Some people find themselves running with only a few others for stretches of the race. All the better for contemplating your beautiful surroundings.

LONDON MARATHON

One of the most jubilant days in London—no crown required

SEASON: Spring   **NO. OF MARATHON RUNNERS:** 48,000   **OTHER RACE DISTANCES:** Kids' mile and 2.6K (1.6 mi)
ELEVATION GAIN/LOSS: 417 feet (127 m)/528 feet (161 m)   **DIFFICULTY:** Easy

The London Marathon is another World Marathon Major. Professional distance runners come here to run exceptionally fast—the world records in the men's and women's divisions have been set here many times. Not only that, but London has a reputation for setting dozens of eclectic Guinness World Records each year, such as the fastest marathon wearing clogs, the fastest marathon with two runners handcuffed together, and the fastest marathon dressed as a fairy-tale character (the list goes on and on—and the people-watching is worthwhile).

The course is made for speed, but you need strategy. Mile three includes a downhill stretch that fools some runners into going faster than they should so early in the race. Resist the urge to leg it out and measure your effort. There's a long way to go, but with such an easy course, the odds are good you could leave London with a new PR.

The course itself is a tourist's dream. It starts in Greenwich Park, where the Greenwich Prime Meridian begins (the line that divides the world into Eastern and Western Hemispheres). At about mile six, the route reaches the *Cutty Sark,* a British clipper ship originally launched in 1869 exclusively for the China tea trade and now a museum. It happens to be one of the most popular points on the course for spectators, so expect a raucous crowd there. Just before the halfway point, you run over the Tower Bridge, one of the most

RACE TIP

It's notoriously difficult to gain entry into the London Marathon. Most apply through the lottery system, but consider that a roll of the dice. If you're an international runner, you will have better luck entering through one of the race's tour operators, or by raising money for one of the official charities.

OPPOSITE: Runners pass Big Ben and the Houses of Parliament at mile 25.

PAGES 174-175: The finish line follows a left turn at Buckingham Palace. Keep an eye out—royals might be watching!

iconic sites in the city, downstream from London Bridge. From miles 14 through 21, participants head through Canary Wharf, the city's financial district as well as an arts hub with plenty of cafés (keep an eye out for where you might want tea at another point in your trip). Though plenty of spectators make their way to this part of the course, the real noise arrives as you pass through Shadwell, part of London's East End.

As you run along the embankment of the River Thames, with about three miles (4.8 km) to go, you'll spot the London Eye to your left, an observation Ferris wheel on the south bank of the river. You'll turn onto Birdcage Walk toward the homestretch—but don't kick just yet! It's still a stretch. Buckingham Palace, the royal residence and administrative headquarters of the monarchy, is just ahead, but the finish is not as close as it looks. When you reach the palace, turn onto the mall to cross the finish line. Members of the royal family have been known to show support from time to time, so keep your eyes peeled for a prince or princess cheering you on.

APRÈS RACE

London's calling with its pubs, restaurants, theater, and more, but it's impossible to do everything *and* run a marathon. If you have limited time, head to the South Bank district between the Westminster and London Bridges. You can take in nice views of Big Ben, St. Paul's Cathedral, and the Tower of London while enjoying street food, arts venues, and good restaurant options.

The secret's out on the appeal of the London Marathon. A record-setting 840,318 applicants sought entry into the field for the 2025 race. The event typically sees about 53,000 finishers, and in 2023 it became the first marathon to give equal prize money to both wheelchair and non-wheelchair athletes.

Aside from the overwhelming crowd support and the chance to see bits of London's history, the event aims to remain one of the largest fundraisers in the world. Runners sign up to support charities of all kinds while training for the marathon. And they take their commitment to the next level on race day, many dressing in costumes that connect to the organization they're representing. One Save the Rhino runner, for example, wore a rhino costume for all 26.2 miles. As of 2024, more than $1 billion had been raised through the London Marathon for various nonprofit organizations.

ABOVE: The podium finishers for the 2023 wheelchair marathon: (L-R) third-place Tomoki Suzuki of Japan, first-place Marcel Hug of Switzerland, and second-place Jetze Plat of the Netherlands

OPPOSITE: Runners cross the Tower Bridge at mile 12.

MAD MARATHON

An idyllic small-town race (with a free hug!)

SEASON: **Summer** NO. OF MARATHON RUNNERS: **300** OTHER RACE DISTANCES: **5K; 10K; half-marathon; marathon relay** ELEVATION GAIN/LOSS: **1,500 feet (457 m)/1,200 feet (366 m)** DIFFICULTY: **Challenging**

The Mad Marathon takes place in Waitsfield, Vermont, in a region known as the Mad River Valley. The quaint town of just about 2,000 residents is tucked between two world-class ski resorts: Sugarbush and Mad River Glen in the Green Mountains. Think covered bridges, dairy farms, maple syrup, and Ben and Jerry's ice cream. It's idyllic, really. In fact, the event's tagline is "the world's most beautiful marathon."

Though the setting is tranquil and full of farmland and mountain vistas, the race still comes with its challenges. In July, humidity levels around 78 percent are not unusual—and the temperature averages 80°F (27°C), though it's just as likely to be cool and misty (New England weather is fickle after all, so prepare for anything). The conditions aren't the only test. The course has a number of hills sprinkled throughout its 26.2 miles. It seems like you're either going up or down the entire way.

You start blissfully in the middle of town on a downhill mile to the Great Eddy Covered Bridge. The covered bridges of New England are historic landmarks, built and enclosed from around 1820 to 1904 to protect the structures from the harsh Northeast weather. Many of the bridges no longer exist, but the Great Eddy is still functional today—and is the oldest operating covered bridge in Vermont.

After enjoying that downhill stretch, you're ready for the first ascent on Joslin Hill Road (you know it's significant if the word "hill" is included in the name). It's about 1.2 miles (1.9 km) to the top, and you'll know that you've reached the apex when you see a large cemetery looming ahead (don't

APRÈS RACE

Nothing is better than ice cream after a summer marathon. As luck would have it, Ben and Jerry's corporate headquarters is less than 30 minutes north of Waitsfield, and you can book factory tours on the company's website. The tour ends in the Flavor Room, where visitors get to taste-test the goods.

The Green Mountains are the constant backdrop of this breathtaking race.

ABOVE: Runners who prefer a Zen-like atmosphere over massive crowds will be right at home at the Mad Marathon.

OPPOSITE: Waitsfield is home to numerous quaint antique shops worth exploring after the race.

worry—it's not a sign!). You'll recover on a downhill that leads to Pine Brook, another covered bridge. At this point, the terrain levels out and sections of the course can be identified by farms along the dirt roads and gravel pathways. You might see more chickens and cows than spectators on some of these stretches, especially near the Von Trapp Farmstead, named for the family made famous by *The Sound of Music*. They settled in Vermont and founded the farm in the 1940s. You can visit the still operational farm before or after the race to load up on cheese, yogurt, and more.

When you've reached the final significant uphill at mile 16, you can take a deep breath and (mostly) roll down to mile 25. But remember that nice descent at the beginning? You'll have to climb it to reach the finish line. There, the race director is waiting for you—as is tradition, she gives each runner a hug.

MARATHON DU MÉDOC

A 26.2-mile wine-tasting party

SEASON: Fall   **NO. OF MARATHON RUNNERS: 8,500**   **OTHER RACE DISTANCES: None**
ELEVATION GAIN/LOSS: Minimal   **DIFFICULTY: Easy**

When you get to the aid stations at the Marathon du Médoc, you'll probably be asked "Red or white?" before you're offered water. This event is a race only by the loosest definition of the term. Really, it's a sprightly jaunt through the Bordeaux region of France, a run between 23 on-course wine stations, as well as stops for fancy cheeses and other gourmet delights like steak, oysters, and foie gras. Few sign up for head-to-head competition or personal records here, unless they're vying for the coveted best costume prize (you'll take home a case of wine if you win). Almost everybody dresses up for this run. From elegant gowns to groups of friends in grape-themed getups, you'll see a bit of everything out there.

If it's not already clear, the Marathon du Médoc has few serious rules. The winners of the men's and women's categories are awarded their weight in Médoc wines (this area is primarily known for its reds, with a focus on cabernet sauvignon). The course winds its way through 59 vineyards in southwest France, beginning in the village of Pauillac on the banks of the Gironde estuary. The route gives participants a chance to see some of the most famous wine estates in the area, including Château Lafite Rothschild (in 2010, an 1869 Lafite broke the world record for the most expensive bottle of wine sold at auction, at $233,973) and Château Latour, one of the oldest continuous

OPPOSITE: Acrobats perform above the starting line as things get going.

PAGES 184-185: Are you spirited enough to stop at one of the race's many wine stations?

Bordeaux winemakers in the region, with a history dating back to the 14th century.

For wine enthusiasts who treasure views of rolling green hills marked by endless tidy rows of grapevines, as well as fairy tale–like châteaus around every bend, the event is a feast for the eyes as much as for the stomach. Each year, organizers select a theme, called the "dress code"— and almost all runners plan their costumes around it. In 2024, the theme was the Olympics to honor the Summer Games held the same year in Paris. The year I participated, the theme was animals, so I showed up in a full-length penguin outfit. The beak and webbed feet made for a cumbersome five-hour run on an 80°F (26.6°C) day, but it was a relief to find that ice cream was being served at kilometer 40. Learn your lesson from me: Choose your attire strategically.

Though the 26.2-mile run is the main event, the Marathon du Médoc is a three-day festival. It begins with a prerace pasta dinner. Not your average carb-loading affair, dinner is served with plenty of wine and the night turns into a dance party, with live music and lots of singing. The day

SOUVENIRS

Once you've tasted the wine in France, chances are you'll want to bring some home. Although some wineries will ship bottles to you, it's pricey. Another option is to bring a wine suitcase with foam inserts and a hard case to protect the bottles, and check it for the flight home.

after the marathon, a three-course lunch is served (more wine, more music, and more dancing), and there is a 10K walk through the Margaux vineyards, with free wine tastings and snacks along the way. Friends and family are invited to both postrace events, but reserve your tickets early because they sell out fast.

The Marathon du Médoc requires a very different kind of recovery than any other event, but it ranks as the truest form of "fun run" you can find.

TRAVEL TIP

Leave time in your itinerary to explore the town of Bordeaux, which is about an hour south of Pauillac. In fact, many people stay in Bordeaux and take advantage of the free race shuttle to the starting line. Bordeaux is filled with museums and stunning 18th-century architecture.

ABOVE: Don't worry about missing the châteaus. Race weekend offers a walking tour of all the vineyards the day following the marathon.

OPPOSITE: Despite its historic setting, this race is far from stuffy.

MISSOULA MARATHON

Paradise found for outdoorsy folk who love to run

SEASON: Summer **TOTAL NO. OF RUNNERS:** 1,500 **OTHER RACE DISTANCES:** Kids' 1.2-mile (1.9 km) run; 3-mile (4.8 km) beer run; 5K; half-marathon **ELEVATION GAIN/LOSS:** 492 feet (150 m)/315 feet (96 m) **DIFFICULTY:** Easy

Runners rave about the hospitality and organization of the Missoula Marathon each year. On the point-to-point course, participants travel westward by bus to the starting line for the 6 a.m. race, then run back to historic downtown Missoula.

The Missoula region, nestled in the Northern Rockies, is considered one of the most picturesque in the Northwest and an outdoor adventurer's dream. The people of Missoula take outdoor recreation to an extreme level—if a marathon isn't enough activity for you, you'll find ample hiking, kayaking, and paddling to stretch your other muscles.

Marathon runners will experience all of Missoula's natural splendor along the route, running through pine forests and tracing a path parallel to the Clark Fork River, a popular and serene destination for fly-fishing. The cool mountain air, in the 40s and 50s Fahrenheit (4–15°C) most mornings, makes for a pleasant run, and the course is mostly flat—the only significant hill comes about halfway through.

Missoula is home to the University of Montana. As runners get closer to the finish, they cross the Beartracks Bridge into downtown, flanked on either side by crowds of cheering spectators, many of them students. The finish line is a small-town festival, offering plenty of food, drinks, and areas to meet up with family and friends in Caras Park.

TRAVEL TIP

Hit Caras Park before the race for a shake-out run, or try the Riverfront Trail, where you can sit back and catch a breath while watching kayakers paddle by.

You'll face two bridge crossings: one around mile 10 and one around mile 15.

KILIMANJARO MARATHON

An epic run circling Africa's famed peak

SEASON: **Southern Hemisphere summer** TOTAL NO. OF RUNNERS: **12,000** OTHER RACE DISTANCES: **5K; half-marathon** ELEVATION GAIN/LOSS: **1,886 (575 m)/1,886 (575 m)** DIFFICULTY: **Moderate**

The very name Kilimanjaro Marathon may scare some people away from giving this race a try, but you won't want to miss this loop on the outskirts of Moshi, Tanzania, the capital of the region. Though run on hard-clay country roads and with a few rolling hills, the course does not include climbing the highest mountain in Africa (though it might inspire your next adventure).

Even so, Moshi sits at 3,120 feet (950 m) above sea level, so runners who aren't acclimated to altitude may feel a little short of breath. And though conditions might be challenging, race attendees exude enthusiasm, with many locals cheering or participating themselves. Organizers call the race a breeding ground for local talent, so you're bound to see fierce competition at the front of the pack.

The event starts and ends at Moshi Stadium and heads southeast along the main road. Then the field turns back toward Mount Kilimanjaro and heads up a long, gradual hill toward Mweka, home of the College of African Wildlife Management. Along the way, participants pass plenty of small farms, cruise by banana and coffee plantations, and run through several small forests.

Tanzania is located south of the Equator. Temperatures on race day in February range from 63° to 85°F (17–30°C). It's usually cooler at the start and heats up quickly throughout the day—so wear layers. The race provides

GEAR CHECK

If you're planning to climb Mount Kilimanjaro, make sure to pack plenty of warm gear, including insulated and waterproof pants, long-sleeved shirts, a waterproof shell jacket, and a fleece top. Layers are critical to weathering extreme conditions from bottom to top (and back down again).

OPPOSITE: Mount Kilimanjaro towers over Moshi, Tanzania.

PAGES 192-193: Wherever the course takes you, the peak remains in sight.

water at aid stations along the way, as well as wet sponges to cool down and oranges for jolts of fuel, but you might consider running with a hydration vest and bringing your own nutrition to ensure you have what you need to complete the distance.

In the closing miles, runners enjoy stretches of downhill and flat terrain. To herald the finish at Moshi Stadium, local bands play and crowds pack the stands to cheer for everybody. One of the race's major sponsors, Kilimanjaro Premium Lager, has cold beer waiting.

One of the major reasons organizers created this race in 2002 was to boost tourism in the region. So after the race, you have one obvious, but bold, option: to climb Mount Kilimanjaro. Most visitors who choose to take on the feat follow the Marangu Route to the 19,340-foot (5,895 m) summit, which is a 50-mile (80 km) round trip. On the way up, you'll experience five ecological climate zones, including the arctic summit.

If you're looking for something more relaxing after your run, consider a safari. Serengeti National Park is easily accessible from this area and offers a high chance of spotting Africa's big five: lions, leopards, elephants, African buffalo, and rhinos. Most runners sign up for the Kilimanjaro Marathon through a tour company, which can arrange a variety of excursions, including tackling the famous peak.

NAPOLI CITY HALF MARATHON

A race worth finishing—you couldn't dream of a better post-run meal

SEASON: Winter   **TOTAL NO. OF RUNNERS: 6,200**   **OTHER RACE DISTANCE: Half-marathon relay**
ELEVATION GAIN/LOSS: Minimal   **DIFFICULTY: Easy**

Lovers of Naples say that the city offers one of the best Italian experiences you can find. It might lack the glam of Milan or the artistry of Florence, but the cobblestone streets, giant castles, and ancient ruins are all worth the trip. And Naples is the birthplace of pizza; its mastery of the dish might just spoil your favorite hometown slice shop by comparison. The wood-fired, pillowy-soft dough, with just enough fresh mozzarella distributed over the tangy red sauce, is part of this city's claim to fame.

But you're also here to run. The Napoli City Half Marathon shows off another reason why the city is a great destination. Imagine running along the seafront with Mount Vesuvius, the volcano that destroyed Pompeii in A.D. 79, as a backdrop. The route also tours through the public square, called the Piazza del Plebiscito. Look also for Castel Nuovo, an imposing medieval castle built in 1279 that now headquarters the Neapolitan Society of Homeland History. Bands play live music along the way and the race ends at the Mostra d'Oltremare (also the start), where finishers are treated to a water display at the Esedra Fountain, timed to classical music.

Known for its stunning Mediterranean views, this race is also a fast one—records in both men's and women's have been set here, so be prepared for fast paces at the front of the pack. For a more laid-back run, consider the relay on the same route.

Catch the colors of a Naples sunrise during a shakeout run.

NEW YORK, NEW YORK, U.S.A.

NEW YORK CITY MARATHON

Run before a crowd of millions in one of the world's most famous races.

**SEASON: Fall   NO. OF MARATHON RUNNERS: 51,000   OTHER RACE DISTANCE: 5K
ELEVATION GAIN/LOSS: 810 feet (247 m)/824 feet (251 m)   DIFFICULTY: Moderate**

If you ever wanted to feel like a celebrity for a day, run the New York City Marathon. Nearly two million people line the entire 26.2-mile course and cheer for each of the 51,000 runners as if that runner alone were winning the race. And participants on any given year hail from 140 different countries. It's the melting pot of marathon running.

On the first Sunday in November, the marathon field takes a ferry or bus to Staten Island for the start. The spectacle as they leave the starting line and cross the Verrazzano-Narrows Bridge is one of the most iconic in American sports. New York Harbor is below, and the Statue of Liberty stands in the distance before the Lower Manhattan skyline. You could almost forget the race starts with an uphill mile until the bridge finally slopes downward into Brooklyn. You have four more bridges to go—and you can think of them each as hills.

You spend nearly half the race in Brooklyn, and the neighborhoods in this borough come out in full force, the brownstone stoops booming with celebrators cheering you on. A highlight of Brooklyn is the raucous party on Lafayette Avenue. The music is loud and the residents louder. Take it all in before you get to the Brooklyn-Queens Expressway. Running through the largely Hasidic Jewish neighborhood of South Williamsburg is a much different vibe—supportive, but in a mellower way.

QUALIFYING

You can qualify for the marathon in several ways. One is by lottery, which you enter in February. Most runners choose the 9+1 program, in which runners complete nine qualifying races and volunteer at one qualifying opportunity in the year prior to the marathon. You can also qualify via charitable components.

OPPOSITE: This is a lively marathon—but the field is also serious and competitive.
PAGES 198-199: The Verrazzano-Narrows Bridge makes an epic beginning to the race.

When you cross the Pulaski Bridge into Queens, you've officially hit the halfway point, and you're gearing up for the Queensboro Bridge, where the lack of spectators means the only sounds you'll hear are footsteps and heavy breathing. Relish that mile or so of precious peace, because when you descend onto First Avenue in Manhattan, the crowd truly goes wild. And this is the point, mile 16, where you can make your biggest mistake of the race—allowing that roar to fuel your adrenaline and boost your speed too soon before your kick. Many runners have covered First Avenue at lightning speed and regretted it somewhere in the Bronx, where you hit mile 20.

Some of the toughest miles are ahead, so the spirit of Harlem couldn't come at a better time. Often a gospel choir sings near Marcus Garvey Park, and the Harlem Run club forms a cheer zone. Then you're off to Fifth Avenue, back into Manhattan for good. Museum Mile is a sneaky hill—you can't see it, but you can feel it—before you pass the Guggenheim and enter Central Park through

PRE-RUN ACTIVITIES

It's easy to get caught up in all the brand-sponsored shakeout runs, panel discussions, and other events surrounding the New York City Marathon—not to mention the limitless options the city itself offers (Broadway shows, Times Square, the Met, and more). Try to save some of these activities for after the race—the city can steal a lot of energy in a short amount of time. Remember that the best tour of New York is the one you'll take on race day.

ABOVE: Streets throughout all five boroughs are blocked off for racers, and New Yorkers come out from all corners to cheer on competitors.

OPPOSITE: More than 51,000 runners finished the marathon in 2023.

Engineers' Gate. After the route through the park, you follow the road down the east side, back onto 59th Street. It's a bit of an uphill stretch to Columbus Circle, where you reenter Central Park on the west side. When you finally reach mile 26, it's just another slight uphill to the finish line, right outside Tavern on the Green, Central Park's iconic restaurant.

Congrats on finishing! This is one of the more challenging World Marathon Majors (with strict qualifiers to compete). Now all you have to do is figure out how to get back to your hotel.

The celebrity treatment will follow you around the city for the rest of the day. When locals see your hard-earned medal, they won't be shy to offer congratulations (and directions) everywhere you go.

PARIS MARATHON

A race through every postcard-perfect scene in the City of Light

SEASON: Spring   **NO. OF MARATHON RUNNERS: 54,000**   **OTHER RACE DISTANCES: None**
ELEVATION GAIN/LOSS: 474 feet (144 m)/443 feet (135 m)   **DIFFICULTY: Moderate**

History, art, fashion, culture: The Schneider Electric Marathon de Paris puts it all on display. A tour of almost all of the city's most notable landmarks makes this one of the most scenic of all the urban races. The Paris Marathon is a loop course that starts and ends on the Champs-Élysées, a picturesque avenue and a shopper's paradise (the Louis Vuitton flagship store is also an art museum). Passing through the Place de la Concorde, the city's major public square, you'll see the Luxor Obelisk and the iconic Fontaine des Mers and Fontaine des Fleuves.

After just the first 10 kilometers, participants will have glimpsed Palais Garnier, the world-famous opera house; the Place du Carrousel public square outside the Louvre Palace; and the Place de la Bastille, where the bastille (prison) once stood. Just past the 10-kilometer mark sits the Château de Vincennes, a medieval castle, home to French kings from the 14th to 16th centuries. On the eastern edge of Paris, the route traces around the Bois de Vincennes, a lovely green space with lakes and trails where residents can escape the urban sprawl.

From the park, the course returns to the city. The next major attraction, just after kilometer 25, is Notre-Dame Cathedral, still undergoing reconstruction after a 2019 fire destroyed part of the roof and spire. Around this point in the race, participants will be carving a path along the River Seine, though

RACE TIP

The Paris Marathon likes to celebrate debutantes to the 26.2-mile distance. If it's your first marathon, your race bib will come in a special golden color to distinguish you as a first-timer. Expect a lot of extra support from the crowd when you're out on the course.

OPPOSITE: Pass by the July Column in the Place de la Bastille, which commemorates the revolution of 1830.

PAGES 204-205: The landmark you've been waiting for, the Eiffel Tower, sits at mile 19.

the course offers a few rolling hills too. After passing the Musée d'Orsay, where you can immerse yourself in Impressionist art on a rest day, you'll be treated to a close-up view of the Eiffel Tower, with just about 10 kilometers to go.

The Auteuil Hippodrome signals that you've made it to the west-end park called Bois de Boulogne. You have a bit more than five kilometers to go before running through the Arc de Triomphe at the top of Champs-Élysées. It's a thrilling finish line (it punctuates the Tour de France as well) and a significant one for the French people. The landmark honors those who fought and died during the French Revolution and Napoleonic Wars.

The Parisian crowds along the way are supportive and numerous—so much so that runners have noted that the combination of narrow roads and lots of spectators can make the path downright constrictive at points. The aid stations serve primarily water and nontraditional fuel like gingerbread slices, dried fruit, sugar cubes, pretzels, and saltine crackers. If you prefer sports drinks and gels, consider carrying a fanny pack.

ON THE COURSE

The race organization behind the Paris Marathon is taking major steps toward eco-conscious sustainability, so runners are not given cups of water at the aid stations like they are at most U.S. races. Rather, you'll receive recyclable bottles. And if you throw warm-up clothes to the side of the road at the start, they will be donated to charity.

ABOVE: Runners start and end along the iconic Champs-Élysées, nicknamed "the world's most beautiful avenue."

OPPOSITE: Racers celebrate their achievement together.

The Paris Marathon features stretches of cobblestone streets. This can be challenging if you have a history of ankle injuries, or prefer a thinner shoe, so anticipate the surface by breaking in a cushiony pair of shoes or bracing your ankles for added stability.

The marathon can be a good opener to a Paris trip, because you can revisit some of your favorite places along the route once you cross the finish line. If more days on your feet sounds tiring, however, take it easy and book a river cruise. Numerous tour companies offer a float down the Seine with dinner and sightseeing. National Geographic Expeditions offers river cruises that make their way from Paris to Normandy, with stops in beautiful hamlets and valleys in between. Whether on water or on land, be sure to refuel after your race with all the delectable French cuisine: buttery croissants, crepes, baguettes with cheese, espresso, wine, steak frites, and more.

PHILADELPHIA MARATHON

The race that follows in Rocky's footsteps

SEASON: Fall   **TOTAL NO. OF RUNNERS: 35,000**   **OTHER RACE DISTANCES: Kids' half-mile and mile; 8K (5 mi);
half-marathon**   **ELEVATION GAIN/LOSS: 744 feet (227 m)/744 feet (227 m)**   **DIFFICULTY: Easy**

The birthplace of the U.S. Constitution is a charming setting for a course that takes participants through a time capsule of American history. The race winds through the heart of the City of Brotherly Love, beginning near the steps of the Philadelphia Museum of Art, most recognizable as the place where Sylvester Stallone's Rocky culminated his training run to the triumphant notes of the movie's soaring theme. The statue of Rocky overlooks the starting line of the marathon. Can you ask for better motivation than the sight of Hollywood's greatest underdog? (Maybe save your own charge up the steps for after the race, though.)

You'll begin the marathon on the Benjamin Franklin Parkway and head toward City Hall, a grand brick, white marble, and limestone building billed as "the nation's most elaborate seat of municipal government." Exciting! History buffs will enjoy the subsequent miles following the route's turn onto Arch Street, where you'll see some of the city's greatest hits, including Chinatown's Friendship Gate, the African American Museum, Benjamin Franklin's grave at the Christ Church Burial Ground, the National Constitution Center, and the United States Mint, before the course loops back and passes Independence Hall and the Liberty Bell. You could easily plan an extra postrace day or two around these historic sites to give them more than just a runner's glance.

OPPOSITE: The race begins with an epic view of downtown from the Benjamin Franklin Parkway.

PAGES 210-211: It's all smiles, even if the legs are starting to get sore.

Soon, participants hit West Philadelphia and University City, home of the University of Pennsylvania. Before mile nine, runners will see the Philadelphia Zoo and the first of the course's rolling hills. The elevation rises and falls as the route travels through Fairmount Park, over the Schuylkill River near the halfway point, and eventually on to Kelly Drive, into a neighborhood called Manayunk. Though the first half of the course might host UPenn students and consistent spectators, Manayunk is probably the rowdiest section—this enclave knows how to throw a party. If you're looking for a beer, it will not be hard to find in Manayunk—celebrators are more than happy to pass them out to passing racers.

Just after mile 20, you'll turn around and head back down Kelly Drive toward the Philadelphia Museum of Art. If you have it in you after you cross the finish line, do your best Rocky impression and climb up those steps to raise your arms in victory.

APRÈS RACE

There are unwritten rules to ordering the iconic Philadelphia cheesesteak sandwich. The two major purveyors in the city are Pat's and Geno's. Locals argue over which is better (and other names, like Tony Luke's, are often thrown into the hat), but you can decide for yourself. Whichever you choose, remember that a "cheesesteak wit" is with onions (for no onions, just say "wit-out"), and you have an option of American cheese, provolone, or melty Cheez Whiz (commonly just called Whiz).

REYKJAVÍK MARATHON

An epic summertime race—with natural hot springs to soothe postrace muscles

SEASON: Summer **NO. OF MARATHON RUNNERS:** 1,000 **OTHER RACE DISTANCES:** 10K; half-marathon
ELEVATION GAIN/LOSS: 571 feet (174 m)/571 feet (174 m) **DIFFICULTY:** Easy

Reykjavík is the northernmost capital in the world, but it's just a six-hour flight from New York and three hours from London. The race date in mid-August ensures that runners enjoy pristine conditions—usually highs in the mid-50s Fahrenheit (around 13°C). It's the ideal way to bridge the spring and fall marathon seasons.

The loop course starting from downtown Reykjavík, near City Hall, is mostly flat, though the second half of the course has some rolling hills. You might not notice the elevation, thanks to stunning views of the Atlantic Ocean, 700,000-year-old Snæfellsjökull Glacier, and Mount Esja (a chain of volcanic peaks that locals call "the Esja").

Expect a lot of crowd support on the sections that pass through residential neighborhoods. The event coincides with Menningarnott (Culture Night), which marks the birthday of Reykjavík and attracts visitors from all over the country. The festival includes fireworks, concerts, art exhibitions, and local fare, including fish stew, arctic char, lamb and beef, waffles, and more. It's the perfect way to celebrate a 26.2-mile finish.

On the course, participants enjoy a tour of the city, the coastline, and a salmon fishing river in the Elliðaárdalur Valley, a hidden gem of a recreational area for relaxing after the race. Most of the route, however, is through city streets, but parts touch narrower urban trails. The landmark buildings on the

OPPOSITE: **Reykjavík sits on the southern shore of Faxaflói Bay.**

PAGES 214-215: **There's a good chance race day will be overcast. Pack long sleeves.**

route include the Höfdi house, where U.S. president Ronald Reagan and U.S.S.R. general secretary Mikhail Gorbachev met in 1986 in a summit to negotiate the Cold War.

If Icelandic history isn't enough, Iceland's plethora of natural hot springs is a huge boon for racers. One of the most popular year-round activities for residents and tourists alike is soaking in the geothermal pools: The island's volcanic activity heats the mineral-rich water underground. The geothermal spa water is said to have regenerative powers because it's rich in silica and sulfur. A soak in these waters is a perfect way to relax after such a long run. Lucky for registered marathoners, every runner receives a free pass to enjoy one of 17 geothermal pools or hot springs in Reykjavík, either on race day or afterward. If you want to up your spa game, consider heading to the Blue Lagoon—one of the most popular attractions in Iceland. It's about 30 miles (50 km) from the city, accessible by car or bus.

TRAVEL TIP

If you're up for more adventure on foot, hiking Mount Esja should be on your itinerary. It's a 20-minute drive to the base. You'll have a choice of which trail to take to "the Stone" at 2,560 feet (780 m) above sea level—either a steeper, shorter route or a longer, more gradual climb. At the top, enjoy gorgeous views of the city and sea.

RIO DE JANEIRO MARATHON

Beautiful beaches will inspire the way, but save some energy for postrace dancing.

SEASON: Southern Hemisphere fall   **NO. OF MARATHON RUNNERS:** 5,000   **OTHER RACE DISTANCES:** 5K; 10K; half-marathon   **ELEVATION GAIN/LOSS:** Minimal   **DIFFICULTY:** Moderate

The early start time and refreshing ocean breezes are welcomed at this race along Rio de Janeiro's southern Atlantic coastline. It might be winter in Brazil, but the temperatures can still reach the upper 80s Fahrenheit (around 31°C). While the course is flat, the heat can make this marathon more of a challenge.

Beginning and ending in the Flamengo neighborhood, the route is made of two out-and-back sections—one to the north and one to the south. Participants run past plenty of Brazil's natural beauty, with the backdrop of the Serra do Mar mountains and the 98-foot (30 m) Christ the Redeemer statue looming on high. The course takes runners along the country's world-famous beaches, including Ipanema and Copacabana. As you run, tick off parts of the city you'll want to enjoy more thoroughly during your postrace visit.

Rio is an exuberant, colorful place where seemingly everybody likes to party. After all, the entire host city of Carnival turns into a giant festival for five days before Lent. That kind of spirit lasts throughout the year. Consider jump-starting your refueling at a *churrascaria,* an all-you-can-eat steak house where servers slice various cuts of meat (as well as more unusual fare, like chicken hearts and liver) onto your plate until you tell them to stop. And while you're in Rio, take in a bit of nightlife if you have it in you—especially some samba music. The rhythm might make you forget those tired legs.

Runners pass the futuristic Museu do Amanhã, aka the Museum of Tomorrow.

ROME MARATHON

One of the most poignant settings for a monumental race

SEASON: Spring   **NO. OF MARATHON RUNNERS: 19,000**   **OTHER RACE DISTANCE: 5K**
ELEVATION GAIN/LOSS: Minimal   **DIFFICULTY: Moderate**

Imagine running through the Eternal City as its residents cheer, "Magnifico!" and "Bellissimo!" The people of Rome indeed find that thousands of people traversing their streets is a magnificent and beautiful sight, and they line the streets to celebrate the runners.

Fittingly, the Rome Marathon begins at the Colosseum. Are you ready for battle? The arena is the first ancient site you'll pass in a city with thousands of years of history. Lucky for you, the marathon route is a tour of much of what's left of ancient Roman civilization. For history-minded runners, it might be hard to put into words what it means to experience a place where much of the Western world's languages, governments, architectural styles, and more are rooted.

The field leaves the Colosseum and passes the Baths of Caracalla, operational until the 530s. Another landmark during this early part of the race is Piramide di Caio Cestio, or the Pyramid of Cestius. The Egyptian-style pyramid was built as a tomb between 18 and 12 B.C. Next, look for the Circus Maximus, an ancient chariot-racing stadium.

Large portions of the route follow the Tiber River, where most of the terrain is flat, though you'll encounter a few hills in the second half of the race. You might be digging deep by this point, but try to keep your eyes up because there's still plenty to see. Just past kilometer 15, runners will glimpse St. Peter's

OPPOSITE: **The Rome Marathon doubles as a celebration in the city's center.**
PAGES 220-221: **Rome's Tomb of the Unknown Soldier sits beneath a statue of the city's deity, the goddess Roma.**

Basilica in Vatican City (the race doesn't enter the small city-state), where St. Peter and many Catholic popes are buried. After a short jaunt around the outskirts of the Holy See, you'll see a giant rotunda: Castel Sant'Angelo. Popes once used it as a fortress and castle, but it was originally intended to be a mausoleum for Roman emperor Hadrian. Today, it's a museum. The top floor offers magnificent postrace views of the city.

Before reaching kilometer 30, the route goes past Ponte Milvio, a bridge spanning the Tiber River that dates back to 206 B.C. When you see the Piazza del Popolo, a large urban square with an ancient obelisk in the center, you have a little more than five kilometers to go. Soon the Colosseum will come back into view, and you'll race toward the finish line at the Imperial Fora, the center of politics in ancient Rome dating back to at least A.D. 113.

The weather in Rome at this time of year is ideal for running. The low temperatures are in the 40s Fahrenheit (4–10°C) and the highs are in the 60s Fahrenheit (15–20°C). Beware that about six kilometers (3.7 mi) of the race are over cobblestone

WHAT TO EAT

Try out a long-held Roman tradition: Gnocchi Thursday, derived from a Catholic practice when the high-calorie dish was prepared on Thursdays before people fasted or ate fish-based meals on Fridays. Nothing will fill those glycogen stores better than potato dumplings smothered in tomato sauce.

roads—for a stretch in the opening kilometers, then again around St. Peter's Basilica, and finally in the final kilometers toward the finish line. The cobblestones underfoot can feel uncomfortable and uneven, especially for runners with sensitive feet, and might lead to muscle soreness by the final few miles. If Rome is your next run of a lifetime, consider breaking in cushioned shoes by race day.

RACE TIP

Many international marathons, including Rome, provide fruit on the course but do not give out other sports nutrition products like gels. The old adage holds true: Don't try anything new on race day! If you're accustomed to gels, be sure to bring them with you. Water and electrolyte drinks are also available in Rome.

ABOVE: Waves in Rome are organized by pace, so you can find camaraderie with those who start alongside you.

OPPOSITE: Runners pass the Colosseum near mile 25.

SHAMROCK MARATHON

A St. Paddy's Day tradition perfect for personal bests and beach lovers

SEASON: Spring   **TOTAL NO. OF RUNNERS:** 20,000   **OTHER RACE DISTANCES:** Kids' mile; 8K (5 mi); half-marathon
ELEVATION GAIN/LOSS: 270 feet (82 m)/272 feet (83 m)   **DIFFICULTY:** Easy

The finish line beer garden at the Shamrock Marathon—a full two city blocks long—is definitely worth running 26.2 miles to get to. This race is an extended celebration of St. Patrick's Day at the beach, so pack your green running apparel and consider a green swimsuit for good measure.

The marathon route is almost perfectly flat, so if you're after a personal record, this is the place to do it (though be aware that the finicky East Coast spring could deliver an ocean headwind). Just set your pace and cruise along the steady, even terrain.

The course circles around Fort Story at miles seven and eight, where Jamestown colonists landed in America in 1607. Along the way, you'll also see the original Cape Henry Lighthouse, the oldest standing lighthouse in the United States. After the field starts heading south (the course is essentially two out-and-back sections), runners will see Camp Pendleton, a military base now used for training the Virginia National Guard, between miles 20 and 21. The finish is on the celebrated Virginia Beach Boardwalk, just past a 26-foot-tall (8 m) bronze statue of King Neptune, lord of the sea.

There are plenty of hotels located within walking distance of the finish, so enjoy the postrace St. Paddy's Day party, which includes food, drinks, and live music. Then soak those tired feet in the nice, cold Atlantic Ocean. Instant relief.

Hard to tell if this is prerace hype or postrace celebrating—but that's the Shamrock Marathon in a nutshell.

ST. GEORGE MARATHON

A downhill treasure that will work those quads

SEASON: **Fall**   NO. OF MARATHON RUNNERS: **5,000**   OTHER RACE DISTANCES: **Kids' mile; 5K; half-marathon**
ELEVATION GAIN/LOSS: **500 feet (152 m)/3,057 feet (932 m)**   DIFFICULTY: **Moderate**

Low humidity, cool mornings, and an extremely (extremely!) downhill course combine for a fast race if you play your cards right. St. George, in the Mojave Desert in the southwestern corner of Utah, is your setting. And the marathon has become a favorite for people looking to clock that personal best time, aided by 12 miles (19 km) of rapid descent at the end of the race. In fact, many come here to run a Boston Marathon (page 112) qualifying time.

Runners arrive early in the morning for the point-to-point trek—buses depart St. George beginning at 3:30 a.m., so set your alarm clock and go to bed early. The race starts in a little town called Central, located 5,197 feet (1,584 m) above sea level. The finish line in St. George, meanwhile, is 2,680 feet (817 m) above sea level. That's quite the drop. Campfires near the start keep you warm while you wait around for the race to begin, and a DJ keeps the energy high.

After the race begins, runners are welcomed with an opening downhill 10K. Careful! It's easy to get ahead of yourself when the terrain feels easy and your legs are fresh. Try to rein it in, because you will have to contend with some sneaky uphills from miles seven through 12. Your quads have a lot of work ahead, so don't tire them out in the first six miles (9.5 km).

The desert landscape is a thing of beauty along the route, as are the Pine

OPPOSITE: Imposing views of Snow Canyon greet runners through the first half of the race.

PAGES 228-229: The open landscape offers incredible views for runners—at least while the sun is up.

Valley Mountains. The red rock formations, cliffs, and mesas are stunning. Visiting city dwellers might be stunned by the wide-open undisturbed landscape. But the expanse has its downside: There's no shade coverage on the course. Lather up with sunscreen around those starting-line campfires and wear a hat on warm, sunny days. Spectators are few and far between until you hit mile 23. Make friends with someone holding your same pace!

After you've screamed down to the finish line, extend your trip to visit Zion National Park, just 30 minutes from St. George. It takes more than a day to experience the entire park, but you can get a taste and stretch your legs at the Emerald Pools and Riverside Walk.

TRAINING TIP

An extremely downhill course requires preparation. Incorporate a hilly route into your training routine and practice proper form: Shorten your strides, lean into the descent from your ankles, and let gravity help you save energy.

STOCKHOLM MARATHON

Where you'll feel like an Olympic champion with a stadium finish

SEASON: Spring   **NO. OF MARATHON RUNNERS:** 15,000   **OTHER RACE DISTANCES:** None
ELEVATION GAIN/LOSS: 866 feet (264 m)/866 feet (264 m)   **DIFFICULTY:** Moderate

The crowds who come out to support the Stockholm Marathon runners like to shout, "Heja! Heja! Heja!" or "Hey! Hey! Hey!" as racers make their way through the city's seven districts. Here, you're in for a thrilling course with a lot of turns and rolling hills through the Swedish capital, comprising 14 islands and 50 bridges on a Baltic Sea archipelago.

Each of Stockholm's seven districts has its own flair and vibe. The race starts and ends in the Östermalm, known for its upscale dining and fashion, as well being home to Sweden's national library and national theater. Next, you enter Vasastan, the northernmost district with Vasaparken, one of the city's most beloved parks. You'll recognize the Stockholm Public Library by its rotunda. Next is Kungsholmen, which is mostly residential but identifiable by City Hall, a Venetian Gothic structure that sits on the water—it hosts the Nobel Prize banquet every year. Runners follow the waterfront to dip into Gamla Stan (Old Town), marked by colorful mustard- and rust-colored buildings. This is also where you'll find the Royal Palace, home of the Swedish Royal Court.

After the race, you should return to the next stop, the Djurgården district, for arts and entertainment (music fans rejoice, for this district features ABBA The Museum, dedicated to the Swedish singing group). For now, conquer

OPPOSITE: The race starts outside Stockholm's Olympic Stadium, where spectators cheer from overpasses.

PAGES 232-233: You'll finish inside the stadium, packed with fans urging you across the line.

the hills en route to Södermalm and brave the Västerbron Bridge, a sizable incline just before kilometer 30. The view from atop the bridge is fantastic. To your right will be another view of City Hall.

The final 10 kilometers lead you to retrace much of the territory you covered in the first half. The finish line is special. You get to run into the Olympic Stadium, opened for the 1912 Summer Games, and finish like a gold medalist. A total of 83 world records have been set here, so you're on sacred running ground. The crowds in the stands will go wild for your achievement.

TRAVEL TIP

Prepare for your circadian rhythm to get a bit off track in Stockholm at this time of year. The sun doesn't set until around 10 p.m., so you may have to trick your body into bedtime. The race does not start until noon, so you can sleep in if the late-night sun prevented shut-eye. If you arrive in Sweden a few days ahead of time, you should be able to get on a schedule and enjoy your time.

SYDNEY MARATHON

Roaring fun, an inclusive atmosphere, and a chance to see the city's sights

SEASON: Southern Hemisphere spring **NO. OF MARATHON RUNNERS:** 17,000 **OTHER RACE DISTANCES:** Sydney Mini Marathon (4.2K/2.6 mi); 10K **ELEVATION GAIN/LOSS:** 889 feet (271 m)/990 feet (302 m) **DIFFICULTY:** Moderate

The Sydney Marathon ensures runners get to experience some of the most popular landmarks of the city. The race begins at the North Sydney Oval, the starting line of the 2000 Olympic marathon. Participants also get to run over the famous Sydney Harbour Bridge. The true highlight, though, is the finish at the majestic Sydney Opera House. It's one of the most recognizable structures in the world, with its shell-shaped rooflines and position on the waterfront. Adjacent to the finish is the Royal Botanic Garden, a beautiful urban oasis worth a postrace visit if your legs can handle it.

The marathon prides itself on being both fun (cheering spectators abound!) and inclusive. Both everyday-use and race wheelchairs are allowed (be sure to sign up for the appropriate wave; race wheelchairs can only compete in the Elite Wheelchair Marathon division). If your family and friends can't make it to the sidelines, they can catch a glimpse on TV or the internet. The Sydney Marathon is the only Australian running event that has a live broadcast.

The weather can be warm on race day, so prepare with a little heat training if you can. For daredevils, the Sydney Harbour Bridge offers another challenge: a bridge climb. In this three-hour tour, you walk the upper arch of the bridge a full 440 feet (134 m) over the water.

There are few better ways to view Sydney's famous harbor than its hometown marathon.

TOKYO MARATHON

The newest major—and one you won't soon forget

SEASON: Spring   **NO. OF MARATHON RUNNERS:** 37,000   **OTHER RACE DISTANCE:** 10.7K (6.6 mi)
ELEVATION GAIN/LOSS: 198 feet (60 m)/322 feet (98 m)   **DIFFICULTY:** Easy

Every year about 300,000 people want to run the Tokyo Marathon, but only 30,000 spots are available through its lottery entry system. The remaining entries are given through fundraising thresholds and qualifying times. It might be harder to register for the marathon than actually run it. But the effort is worth it. This race rewards its participants with a fantastic experience.

The Tokyo Marathon was added to the World Marathon Majors race series in 2012. Ever since, it has garnered accolades from runners for its superb race-day organization and the kindness of its locals. Locals come out in big crowds to support the event, either as volunteers or as spectators. But don't expect the kind of screaming and cowbell ringing you hear at U.S. races. Though spectators cheer, they aren't quite as boisterous as you typically see at races in other parts of the world.

Tokyo is known for its convenient transportation systems, and the start—near the Tokyo Metropolitan Government Building in Shinjuku—is easily accessible by Metro. Make sure you know which line you're taking and at what time you need to leave well ahead of race day (some runners take a "dry run" beforehand to make sure they have it figured out). Many marathoners opt to stay in hotels closer to the finish line so they don't have to walk far after the run. Tokyo temperatures this time of year are cool, usually in the 50s

EATING ON THE RUN

In many ways, Japanese food is a runner's dream. Sushi is the perfect combination of carbs and protein before or after the race. Ramen or soba noodles and *okonomiyaki* (savory pancakes often filled with seafood) are all great choices while you're preparing to run 26.2 miles.

OPPOSITE: The marathon begins in Nishi-Shinjuku, Tokyo's skyscraper district.

PAGES 238-239: World record holders compete in the race's wheelchair division. In 2024, Marcel Hug of Switzerland set a new race record, finishing with a time of 1:15:33.

Fahrenheit (10–15°C), so if your body runs cold at baseline, it might be wise to finish close to a hot shower.

The course is flat, with just a bit of almost unnoticeable elevation gain in the second half. The opening miles are crowded—but the congestion is actually a blessing in disguise, because those first few miles are downhill, and the pack will keep you from starting out too fast. Tuck in and know that the hordes will thin as you progress through the first 5K.

The route is a series of out-and-back sections, which give participants the chance to see one another along the way, and at certain points maybe catch a glimpse of the elites at the front. The course mostly runs through the cityscape, but you'll also get an opportunity to see a couple of Tokyo's notable landmarks. Around the 20-kilometer mark, look for the Kaminarimon Gate of Sensoji Temple, Tokyo's oldest established temple at more than 1,400 years old. Near the finish line at Tokyo Station, the railway hub that connects the city to the rest of Japan, you'll see the Imperial Palace, the residence of the emperor

SPECTATING TIP

The subway system in Tokyo makes watching the race from multiple vantage points feasible. You can get from one end of the course to the other by Metro, and volunteers are stationed to point you in the right direction. The race website also has a detailed map that includes landmarks, road closures, and public transit stops.

ABOVE: Tokyo's nightlife offers a high-energy way to burn off your runner's high.

OPPOSITE: About 37,000 runners compete at this World Marathon Major.

of Japan. With a public park and gardens surrounding the residence, this is also a nice spot for a shakeout run before the marathon. You can follow a 5K loop for the perfect easy jog.

The Tokyo event is also known for its inclusivity, including both a general and an elite wheelchair division as part of the 10.7K race, which also features divisions for those with visual impairments, with intellectual disabilities, and who have had organ transplants. All of these divisions have a women's, a men's, and a nonbinary wave. While 37,500 runners compete in the marathon, the 10.7K field is limited to 500.

The last race mile is usually packed with spectators, so relish the support in your final strides.

TORONTO WATERFRONT MARATHON

Chase the CN Tower along Lake Ontario.

SEASON: Fall   **TOTAL NO. OF RUNNERS: 25,000**   **OTHER RACE DISTANCES: 5K; half-marathon**
ELEVATION GAIN/LOSS: Minimal   **DIFFICULTY: Easy**

When visitors recall their trips to Toronto, they almost universally say, "It's such a beautiful city." The Toronto Waterfront Marathon shows off why. The race makes its way through the heart of Toronto, including more than a dozen different neighborhoods and—as the name might suggest—a majority stretch along the Lake Ontario waterfront (this section can be quite breezy at times—layer up!). The city is almost entirely flat, and race season brings crisp, cool fall conditions, so this event is a good one if you're looking for a fast time.

The start and finish are located at City Hall, a unique landmark with two curved towers that rise to different heights with a saucer-shaped council chamber between them. Around mile 18 you'll skirt past Coronation Park on the shoreline, which marks the spot where King George VI was crowned and also serves as a veterans' memorial today. When you close in on the final 10K or so, keep your eyes on the CN Tower, the most prominent structure of the Toronto skyline.

After the race, Toronto has a lot to offer: The CN Tower has an observation deck with a lookout over the city that's worth a trip before or after the race. Take a 15-minute ferry to Toronto Island Park. The islands in the park—including Centre, Ward's, and Algonquin—are car free, so they are nice places to stroll and see English cottages and gardens.

The course runs through many green spaces in downtown Toronto, including York Mills Valley Park and Alexander Muir Memorial Gardens.

ROYAL VICTORIA MARATHON

A marathon on Canadian Thanksgiving that you'll be grateful for finishing

SEASON: Fall   **TOTAL NO. OF RUNNERS:** 9,000   **OTHER RACE DISTANCES:** 5K; 8K (5 mi); half-marathon
ELEVATION GAIN/LOSS: 790 feet (240 m)/791 feet (241 m)   **DIFFICULTY:** Moderate

Victoria is an outdoor enthusiast's city. Located on the southern end of Vancouver Island, it's the craggy tip of Canada jutting into the Salish Sea. The city boasts that it's "a place where sustainability, health, and well-being are the cornerstones of creating a prosperous and inclusive future." In other words, it's a perfect setting for a marathon.

The Royal Victoria Marathon is known for its hills. Although none of the ascents are massive by most marathon standards, they are, nonetheless, constant. Don't be deterred from pursuing this race, however. It's one of the most scenic in the world, and well worth the effort.

The course begins in the Inner Harbour at the legislative grounds, which are marked by the British Columbia Parliament Buildings, stately classical Renaissance structures. The Empress hotel also serves as a majestic backdrop to the scene. Many runners opt to stay at the hotel—or at least visit for an elegant prerace or postrace brunch or high tea.

The route continues through downtown Victoria and into Beacon Hill Park, which will no doubt be ablaze with autumn colors at this time of year. It proceeds down to the coastline for nine kilometers (5.6 mi) for a small section, until turning again to neighborhood streets, where participants enjoy encouragement from copious spectators celebrating the race *and* a long

OPPOSITE: The fall weather in Victoria is ideal for running.

PAGES 246-247: The impressive British Columbia Parliament Buildings mark both the starting and finish lines of the race.

Canadian Thanksgiving holiday weekend. Runners then circle Oak Bay, an upscale part of Victoria known for art galleries, boutiques, and cafés, and head to the 25-kilometer turnaround point in Uplands, known for luxury homes, its proximity to downtown, and a beautiful waterfront.

From Uplands, you retrace your steps back to Beacon Hill Park, but at the 39-kilometer point, you'll diverge from the beaten path to James Bay—known for its Victorian-style homes and kiosks selling fish-and-chips (you're going to be tempted, but don't stop now!). After just two miles (3.2 km), the Parliament Buildings come back into view and you're crossing the finish line at the picturesque Inner Harbour.

If the serene water vistas aren't enough scenery, runners also get peeks of western Washington State's Olympic Mountains in the distance. You'll also run by Ogden Point and its Breakwater Lighthouse.

Don't forget to save time before or after the race to visit the Terry Fox statue at the Mile 0 monument, near Beacon Hill Park. Fox was a

TRAVEL TIP

Don't miss Butchart Gardens in Brentwood Bay, a magical 55 acres (22 ha) containing 900 varieties of plants. The gardens began in 1904 as a passion project by Jennie Butchart, and though originally meant for family and friends to enjoy, they now draw a million visitors each year. Butchart Gardens has been named a national historic site in Canada.

ABOVE: **More than 1,600 winsome volunteers encourage 9,000 runners of all distances along the course.**

OPPOSITE: Beacon Hill Park distinguishes kilometers four through eight, and you'll double back across the green space for kilometer 37.

celebrated Canadian athlete who, in 1980, set out to run a "Marathon of Hope" from east to west across Canada to raise money for cancer research, after his own leg was amputated due to a cancer diagnosis at age 18. Fox's journey came to a sudden end after 143 days and 3,339 miles (5,373 km) when he was forced to stop running because of a new bout of cancer, this time in his lungs. He died in 1981 at age 22. Since then, runners have continued to raise millions of dollars in his name for cancer research at marathons around the world.

APRÈS RACE

Although the official Canadian Thanksgiving observance is Monday, many host their holiday meals on Sunday evening. These feasts mirror those of the traditional U.S. Thanksgiving, highlighted by turkey and lots of starchy side dishes. It's the ideal way to cap off a race day.

PART THREE

TRAIL RACES & ULTRAS

The Dipsea Race (page 272) in Northern California runs 7.4 miles (11.9 km) from Mill Valley to Stinson Beach.

COMRADES MARATHON

A special race with a spiritual history known for its Ups and Downs

SEASON: **Southern Hemisphere winter**   TOTAL NO. OF RUNNERS: **25,000**   RACE DISTANCE: **Variable, but approximately 55 miles (88.5 km)**   ELEVATION GAIN: **1,200 meters (3,937 ft) on up years, 1,900 meters (6,234 ft) on down years**   DIFFICULTY: **Challenging**

They call it the world's most famous ultramarathon. They also call it the "ultimate human race." In reality, Comrades is an event that is sometimes hard to capture in words. For some, it's a spiritual experience.

What makes Comrades so special? It's steeped in tradition (it started in 1921) as well as love, care, and encouragement of every participant—from the front of the pack to the back. The entire course is lined with locals who want nothing more than for each and every runner to enjoy each and every step.

The race is a point-to-point course, but it runs in one of two directions depending on the year. On "Up" years, the race begins in Durban on the coast and finishes in Pietermaritzburg at 2,218 feet (676 m) above sea level. "Down" years go the opposite way. In either scenario, the marathon is extremely challenging, featuring five major hills: Cowies, Fields, Botha's, Inchanga, and Polly Shortts. And those are just the hills with names. More than 50 percent of runners finish within the last hour of the strict 12-hour cutoff, according to the race website. In other words, it's not a race for the faint of heart (or those who don't like climbing).

At the start of Comrades, the crowd sings "Shosholoza," a song that Black South Africans sang as they came home from working in the mines and later

RACING ADVICE

Half the field finishes Comrades within the last hour of the 12-hour cutoff. That's about a 13-minute-per-mile pace for 55 miles (88.5 km). Every second counts as time starts when the gun goes off, not when you cross the starting line.

OPPOSITE: Comrades attracts a field of thousands, including the world's best ultrarunners, seeking to conquer the course.

PAGES 254-255: The race begins at Durban City Hall.

as an anthem during the fight against apartheid. It's an emotional moment for many Black runners at the starting line, some of whom have said that Comrades race day was the only day of the year during apartheid years that they felt free. After "Shosholoza," the *Chariots of Fire* theme is played, and then the cock crows—well, sort of. In 1948, instead of firing a starter gun, the race official imitated a cock's crow. The tradition continues today—that original official's recorded voice is played over the loudspeaker and, after the gun, away you go.

The highest point on the course is 2,850 feet (870 m) above sea level—kilometer six on an Up year; on a Down year, it's around kilometer 24. The route has many landmarks, too, including the Comrades Marathon Wall of Honour, located where the road overlooks the Valley of a Thousand Hills. It commemorates runners who have finished Comrades, and you can purchase a block for yourself to live on in perpetuity. At a spot about halfway on the Down course is Arthur's

TRAVEL TIP

Durban is a coastal city on the Indian Ocean. Less well known than Cape Town and Johannesburg (both short flights away), it offers plenty of interesting activities that make it a worthwhile stopover. Mahatma Gandhi lived in Durban for 20 years, and his former home is a museum that details his life in South Africa. Not far from there, you can also see where Nelson Mandela placed his vote in South Africa's first democratic elections, in 1994.

ABOVE: **Alexandra Morozova of Russia won the women's division in 2022.**

OPPOSITE: **Comrades' impressive challenge is not lost on the locals.**

Seat, purportedly the favorite resting spot of Arthur Newton, a five-time winner of the race in the 1920s. As the legend goes, runners who greet or place a flower at Newton's seat will have a strong second half. So, don't take any chances.

You'll pass by a number of breathtaking natural landmarks along the route, including a deep ravine formed by the Molweni Stream in the Krantzkloof Nature Reserve. And after conquering a steep and punishing ridge, your efforts will be paid off with sweeping views of the Valley of a Thousand Hills.

Comrades brings runners together with special moments and a chance to become part of its long history. It's humbling, and for some people, it's a life-altering experience. It's no wonder so many people come back time and again, despite how demanding the run is. What goes up must eventually come down too.

ANTARCTICA MARATHON

A once-in-a-lifetime race—among penguins!

SEASON: Southern Hemisphere summer **TOTAL NO. OF RUNNERS:** 360 **RACE DISTANCES:** Half-marathon; marathon
ELEVATION GAIN: Varies by year **DIFFICULTY:** Challenging

S ummer in Antarctica is like winter in Chicago. So though this race is the opportunity of a lifetime, it's also a brutal experience.

The Antarctica Marathon was created by the CEO of Marathon Tours & Travel, a running events tour operator that still owns and organizes the run. The tour company selects a small group to compete each year, and also offers a half-marathon option. For those who've set a goal to run a marathon on each continent, this is your chance to check off the seventh.

Traveling to the race is part of its allure. Runners meet in Buenos Aires, Argentina, for a few days to prepare for the journey. From there, it's a flight to Ushuaia, at the southern tip of South America. Then the group boards a ship for a two-and-a-half-day journey that includes crossing the Drake Passage—a super rough stretch of sea known for high swells and causing seasickness. (Talk with a trusted medical professional beforehand about motion-sickness patches or other medication.) When you finally arrive at King George Island, you just have to hope that Mother Nature plays nice. Often the conditions in Antarctica, even in summer, are as harsh as you'd imagine—snowy, windy, and cold.

The course is marked by flags and mile markers over rolling hills and dirt roads that connect the dozen research bases, home to the island's only

OPPOSITE: Antarctica's landscape can be hostile, even in the summer. To train for the intense cold, some runners set up treadmills in industrial freezers.

PAGES 260-261: In the desolation of Antarctica, camaraderie is welcome and running packs often form.

human inhabitants. In 2024, the route began and ended near Bellingshausen, the Russian base, and passed through the Chilean, Chinese, and Uruguayan bases. The runners ran this loop three times. The course can change from year to year depending on whether a base gives permission for the event. Other variables include weather, but almost without fail, racers face slick conditions and tricky footing over the glacier-carved terrain.

Although you won't have the opportunity to meet many humans aside from your competition, you might get to see some penguins and whales while in Antarctica. After the race, the ship heads to the Antarctic Peninsula and Paradise Bay. Think glaciated mountains, icebergs, and more penguins. Indeed, the marathon is only a small fraction of the experience, but if you're going to Antarctica, wouldn't you want to run 26.2 miles while you're there?

TRAVEL TIP

Packing for this particular marathon is tricky. The temperature and weather conditions can fluctuate wildly during the race, so think about dressing in layers you can shed progressively, with a waterproof layer on top in case of rain or snow. You may also consider some type of traction, such as MICROspikes, to attach to your shoes. Many outdoor companies sell them specifically for runners.

CALICO TRAIL RUN

A ghost-town race and camping trip all in one

SEASON: Winter   **TOTAL NO. OF RUNNERS:** 150   **RACE DISTANCES:** 30K (18.6 mi); 50K (31 mi)
ELEVATION GAIN: 3,670 feet (1,119 m)   **DIFFICULTY:** Moderate

Just 10 miles northeast of Barstow, California, is a place called Calico Ghost Town. As the name implies, it's an old, possibly haunted locale that would be the perfect setting for a black-and-white Western movie. Calico was founded in 1881 as a silver mining hub. However, the town was soon abandoned in the mid-1890s when silver lost value. Today, it's a San Bernardino County regional park and home to the start of an epic trail race.

Don't let the desert setting fool you: January in Yermo is cool and sometimes even cold, with temperatures usually in the 40s Fahrenheit (4–9°C) on race day. Don't worry about shivering, however. You'll heat up thanks to the dirt roads, rugged trails, and intense climbing. The steep canyon downhills in the run's second half will test your concentration too. Loose rock can be unforgiving—and watch out for cacti on the trail's edge.

Before heading back into Calico Ghost Town for the finish line, participants have to battle three miles (4.8 km) of seemingly endless rolling hills. On the upside, you're treated to a run through an actual old mining cave—an experience you won't find anywhere else.

Although Barstow has plenty of hotels, many trail runners opt for camping within the park (showers are available at official campgrounds). Imagine sitting by a campfire swapping tales about race day—and maybe a few ghost stories too.

A bullet-riddled sign greets runners en route to Calico Ghost Town. That'll calm your nerves on race day!

CATALINA ISLAND MARATHON

A fun Cali-style race in an idyllic setting

SEASON: **Spring** TOTAL NO. OF RUNNERS: **1,250** RACE DISTANCES: **5K; 10K; marathon**
ELEVATION GAIN: **4,310 feet (1,314 m)** DIFFICULTY: **Challenging**

Catalina Island is about 22 miles (35 km) off the coast of Southern California. To get there, you have to ride a ferry from Long Beach, San Pedro, or Dana Point (or, for a significantly larger fee, you can take a helicopter). Once in Avalon, the hub of Catalina Island, you're in for white sand beaches, plentiful palm trees, and an absolutely gorgeous marathon.

The race begins on a grassy field on the opposite side of the island from Avalon, in Two Harbors, the only incorporated city on the island (most people stay in Avalon and take a 5 a.m. boat to the start). The starting line used to be a grass runway for small planes, so it feels roomy, but don't get comfortable—after the field, the course narrows quickly to a single-track trail. Then the climbing begins. You'll go up more than 800 feet (240 m) in the first 2.5 miles (4 km). Mile eight will come as respite—it's a small taste of being at actual sea level—before you embark on nearly 15 miles (24 km) of ascent on dirt fire roads (watch out for the "Catalina Crush," mile 19). The highest point on the course is mile 23, which is 1,800 feet (550 m) above sea level. From there, you can see where the finish line awaits in Avalon. Blessedly, you finish on paved roads, where crowds gather to cheer you on until the end.

Spring weather on Catalina Island is variable. Some years the race has been run in a deluge and the roads turn to muddy streams. Other years,

OPPOSITE: **For the marathon, runners traverse the entire length of Catalina Island.**

PAGES 266-267: **Picturesque Avalon Bay, at the foothills of emerald mountains, is peppered with sailboats.**

temperatures have made sections of the island's interior brutally hot. Sometimes, of course, the race is on a perfect California day. Be prepared for just about anything.

No matter the weather or your state amid the hills, don't forget to look around. The ocean vistas are second to none, and you might encounter an American bison or two. The local bison are non-native descendants of a herd left on the island by a movie crew in the 1920s. Today, the Catalina Island Conservancy protects the bison and the rest of Catalina's landscape. The race is part of that effort. The conservancy asks race officials to keep cups off the course, so all participants can purchase a reusable, soft collapsible cup to fill at aid stations, or use their own hydration vest or hand-held bottle.

Catalina Island offers a lot for tourists: loads of outdoor recreation, 7,000 years of history that includes pirates and gold diggers, refreshing sea excursions, and rugged land expedition tours (though the latter might be redundant with the marathon). Take a glass-bottom boat tour onto

TRAINING TIP

Practice your hydration routine during long runs. Because the Catalina Island Marathon is a cupless race, plan to carry water or other fluids on race day. Run with a bottle while training to see how you feel holding it, or wear a hydration vest to test its weight across your body. Once you have your preference, don't leave home without it.

the Pacific Ocean: You might see dolphins and sea lions. Or if you'd rather get a little more up close with the marine life, book a tour on the Sea Wolf Semi-Submersible, which takes you five feet (1.5 m) below the surface. If you prefer dry land, the town of Avalon is a worthwhile jaunt for its charming history, shops, and cafés. Or if the run wasn't thrilling enough, get more adrenaline pumping with an eco-zipline tour above Descanso Beach Club.

ABOVE: Visit the Catalina Casino, on the tip of the bay, for live events on the top floor.

OPPOSITE: You'll gain 4,310 feet (1,314 m) of elevation throughout the course, so enjoy those downhills while you can.

WHERE TO STAY

Most people visiting Catalina Island stay in the beautiful hotels of Avalon, along the beach. If you're hoping for more adventure, however, camping is an option. Or try booking a place in Two Harbors—but plan early because options are limited.

MARATHON DES SABLES

Eleven days of Moroccan adventure built into the race of a lifetime

---

SEASON: Spring   **NO. OF RUNNERS: 1,000**   **RACE DISTANCES: 70–120K (43.5–74.5 mi); 250K (155 mi)**
ELEVATION GAIN: Varies by year; past races have had as much as 6,890 feet (2,100 m)   **DIFFICULTY: Challenging**

The Marathon des Sables is one of the most difficult races in the world. Though the route of this six-stage race changes from year to year—sometimes a stage is 30 kilometers (18.6 miles) in one day, sometimes it's 90 kilometers (60 miles) in two days—the concept has remained the same since 1986: a 250K ultramarathon crossing the Sahara. Runners traverse sand dunes and salt plains on their own, carrying their clothes, food, and supplies to communal tents and water rations the race organization provides. Runners tend to themselves and lean on their personal preparation while traversing some of the harshest conditions in the world. (Especially anxious runners should be comforted: Medical staff checks in with participants every five miles [8 km] or so to ensure each runner is OK to continue.)

Temperatures in the Sahara can reach 122°F (50°C), and the potential for sandstorms is omnipresent, with winds sometimes whipping up to 50 miles an hour (80 km/h). But the race organizers will help you prepare. Each participant receives a long checklist of required equipment, an antivenom pump for encounters with snakes or scorpions, and a compass.

Runners call the Marathon des Sables the ultimate test of self-sufficiency. Beyond that, the camaraderie built at each night's camp forges lifelong friendships.

Bring gaffer tape to wrap and seal your gaiters to your shoes. You don't want to carry any part of the dunes with you.

DIPSEA RACE

A beautiful route and a race anyone can win

SEASON: **Spring** TOTAL NO. OF RUNNERS: **1,500** RACE DISTANCE: **7.4 miles (11.9 km)**
ELEVATION GAIN: **2,200 feet (671 m)** DIFFICULTY: **Challenging**

Since 1905, the Dipsea has served as one of the country's most unique trail races. Runners navigate the old stone steps of the Dipsea Trail in Northern California and some grueling climbs up other steep trails. It's a challenging course, but anyone can win thanks to a unique handicap system that allows certain runners a head start based on gender and age. Almost every year at Dipsea, the top 10 finishers come from different start groups, so keep an eye on who you might be able to catch and who in later groups might try to make a charge.

The Dipsea course from Mill Valley to Stinson Beach is one of the most beautiful routes a trail runner can enjoy. But it isn't easy—these climbs have stairs. The first set of stairs is as tall as a 50-story building, according to race officials. The top landing brings you to picturesque Muir Woods, but you won't have a ton of time to enjoy the scenery. Another climb awaits via a pair of vicious trails named Dynamite and Cardiac. At the top of the aptly named Cardiac portion (be mindful of your pace!), you'll have a quick respite of flat terrain before you're bombing downhill over rocks and roots—a section known as the Steep Ravine. Don't settle into the descent, though. Adding insult to injury, you have another climb up aptly named Insult Hill before sweet relief comes in the form of a gentle downhill grade toward the ocean. Run hard toward the finish line—you never know who you might beat.

Few trails pack in such a wide variety of terrain and landscape in such a short time. Redwoods, creeks, and oceanside trails—Dipsea offers a little bit of everything to everyone—including a chance at the podium.

The final few miles of Dipsea are practically a plummet to the finish.

HOOD TO COAST RELAY

The world's most epic baton exchange leads to a lot of camaraderie.

SEASON: **Summer**   TOTAL NO. OF RUNNERS: **1,000 teams**   RACE DISTANCE: **196 miles (315 km)**
ELEVATION GAIN: **None**   DIFFICULTY: **Moderate**

What's better than a dozen friends, two vans, and endless miles of open Oregon road? The Hood to Coast Relay begins at the Timberline Lodge of Mount Hood and travels 196 miles to Seaside Beach, where runners reunite with their entire team to cross the finish line together on the shore of the Pacific Ocean.

Each relay team has 12 members who take turns running 36 segments (relay legs) of the course. You can strategize who does which legs according to the difficulty levels established by the race officials: Legs are rated easy, moderate, hard, and very hard. Teams plan their race, then split into two vans (you need to reserve rental vans on your own, so do it early—around 1,000 teams are vying for vehicles). The vans correlate with specific chunks of the race, and they leapfrog each other to give half the team a break while the other half continues the run. The runners meet near the end of leg 36 in Seaside for the team finish.

By the end of the relay, each runner will have contributed about 17 miles (27.4 km) and, thanks to runs that take place throughout the night and plenty of loopy midnight-hour van rides, will have made plenty of memories along the way. Hilarity can ensue when two sleep-deprived runners try to pass batons to each other in the middle of the night. As you traverse populated areas along the way, like Portland and Scappoose, local residents and run

TRAINING TIP

All-night relays require you to run in the dark. Practice running with a headlamp ahead of time, as some runners can find it disorienting at first. Experiment with different headlamps to see which one feels most comfortable and offers the best light. In general, you want a model with a wide, bright beam.

OPPOSITE: Though one runner completes the final leg of the relay, the entire team crosses the finish line together.

PAGES 276-277: Most of the relay takes place on paved roads.

clubs come out to support racers, often offering warm food and beverages for sale to support charities. Some stops offer showers. We strongly advise you take a shower whenever possible. Your van mates will thank you.

One of the best enduring Hood to Coast traditions involves decorating your team vans with washable markers (race organizers ask that you keep the jokes family-friendly). Make sure to recruit a creative and artistic runner to your team so your design has pop. In terms of assigning roles, it helps to have a relay captain who can take the lead on planning and organization. Having a type A personality to keep everyone on track, assign vans, remind people of upcoming legs, and supervise logistics is a lifesaver. As for van drivers, some teams opt to drive themselves, but if you have nonrunning friends willing to chauffeur, the trip can be easier on tired racers. The right driver can keep the energy up in the early mornings and evenings, play the perfect song to hype you up for your next leg, or make conversation you'll remember after the finish line. Plus, even the best of us can get lost. A go-to navigator helps ensure they'll be no disasters on race day.

The camaraderie and adventure of the Hood to Coast Relay is second to none. Working as a team comes with a special sense of accomplishment, and crossing that finish line with runners you've passed the baton between is a moment you'll remember forever.

ICE AGE TRAIL 50

A trek through geological eras and time

SEASON: Spring   **TOTAL NO. OF RUNNERS: 1,000**   **RACE DISTANCES: Half-marathon; 50K (31 mi); 50 miles (80.5 km)**
ELEVATION GAIN: 5,000 feet (1,520 m)   **DIFFICULTY: Challenging**

About 10,000 or so years ago, a massive ice sheet blanketed much of Wisconsin. When the ice retreated, it left behind an astonishing landscape: towering deciduous forests, ridges against open prairies and lush valleys, sparkling lakes, and ethereal anomalies known as erratics (rocks and boulders dropped in seemingly random places as glaciers traveled). The Ice Age Trail, where this race takes place, showcases the story of this incredible geological event over the course of its 50 miles. (There are also half-marathon and 50K options.)

The race begins and ends at the Nordic trailhead, north of the town of La Grange. You start with about nine miles (14.5 km) on a Nordic skiing trail before you hit the Ice Age Trail, which is a single-track. Keep an eye on your footing for most of the race—rocks and roots are everywhere, as well as gravel. Many of the trail stretches are runnable, but some participants opt to save energy by hiking the hills on the route. After a turnaround at Rice Lake, runners will reach the highest point on the course after mile 34 on Bald Bluff. The summit was once a gathering spot for Native American spiritual ceremonies.

The terrain from start to finish at the Ice Age Trail 50 is constantly changing, and the climbs are difficult, but the race maintains a community feel to motivate. Volunteers serve the same aid stations year after year—some even travel from other states—and by this point in the Ice Age Trail 50's history, they probably know what you need before you do. Repeat runners often build relationships with the volunteers too.

The 50-mile (80.5 km) trail is mostly single-track dirt through forests and rolling prairie.

IMOGENE PASS RUN

A grueling run for true adventure seekers

SEASON: Late summer   **TOTAL NO. OF RUNNERS:** 1,200   **RACE DISTANCE:** 17.1 miles (27.5 km)
ELEVATION GAIN: 5,600 feet (1,707 m)   **DIFFICULTY:** Challenging

When you're standing at the starting line in Ouray, look up. And up. And up. Eventually you'll spot it: the top, aka Imogene Pass, in the San Juan Mountains. This is your landmark for the first half of the race, but it's not your final destination. After reaching the pass, the run continues down the other side of the mountains until you enter Telluride. But in that moment at the starting line, looking up, it might seem like you've signed up for something nearly impossible.

The Imogene Pass Run has no false advertising. Its tagline is direct and succinct: "A difficult race for well-prepared athletes." The point-to-point course climbs 5,600 feet (1,707 m) to Imogene Pass, which sits 13,114 feet (3,997 m) above sea level. The route runs on a dirt road, a relic of the mining days of the 1800s. The climb is significant: 10 miles (16.1 km) up to the pass, then 7.1 miles (11.4 km) down Tomboy Road to the finish.

For the first six miles (9.7 km), you'll enjoy running mostly through conifer forest. When you exit the trees, you'll see the lower portion of the Imogene Basin before climbing across an avalanche slope to Imogene Creek, which runs along a blasted-out cliff from the mining years. The course requires you to cross the creek, but the water level is typically quite low, and wooden planks are erected for bold runners to hop to the other side. Just before mile eight, you'll hit the Upper Camp Bird aid station—the mandatory turnaround

OPPOSITE: The path between the mountain towns of Ouray and Telluride is exactly what you'd expect in the Rockies.

PAGES 282-283: The aid station around mile 10 rests at the summit of Imogene Pass, the highest point in the race, more than 5,000 feet (1,520 m) above the starting line.

IMOGENE PASS
ELEV 13114 FT

611

YOU ARE AT
IMOGENE PASS STATIO
Mile 10.05   13,120 ft. Elevation

1.90 Miles to Tomboy Station
7.05 Miles to Telluride Finish
4300 Feet of Descent to Telluride

point in bad weather conditions, or for those who have not made the cutoff time.

Here, you'll finally clear the top of the tree line. On a favorable day, with no precipitation, you'll enjoy glorious vistas. You have 1,885 feet (575 m) left to climb, in just 2.4 miles (3.9 km), to Imogene Pass. The sounds of the party at the summit will urge you onward. If you look up during the climb, you'll see runners ahead disappearing one by one over the crest of the trail. When you make it there yourself, you'll understand what all the fuss is about. It feels like you're on top of the world.

At the summit, volunteers serve hot broth, and a line of runners take selfies at the Imogene Pass sign, even if the weather isn't cooperating. Whether your summit stay is short or long, you still have to tumble all the way down to Telluride, where another party awaits.

As you near the finish line, spectators line the streets and hand out beers and Bloody Marys. Once the party has ended, Telluride will be ready to show you a good time now that you've passed the Imogene test.

WEATHER WATCH

The Imogene Pass Run is always held on the cusp of fall. The weather on any mountain is unpredictable, so make sure to have a waterproof layer, gloves, and a hat should the clouds move in and the wind kick up. As of 2023, foul weather has never canceled the race, so prepare to tough out harsh conditions (though if things are truly unsafe, organizers insist they will end the race at the cutoff point so everyone can make it back to Ouray safely).

JUNGFRAU MARATHON

Enjoy a cowbell serenade as you make your way up The Wall.

SEASON: Late summer **NO. OF MARATHON RUNNERS: 4,000** **RACE DISTANCES: Half-marathon; marathon**
ELEVATION GAIN: 6,407 feet (1,953 m) **DIFFICULTY: Challenging**

The Jungfrau Mountains are in the Bernese Oberland region of the Swiss Alps. If you're a mountain lover, this is your ideal marathon. The race begins in Interlaken, in central Switzerland, with a backdrop of Jungfrau—one of three iconic peaks in this region, alongside Mönch and Eiger. This course takes you into view of all three, as well as beautiful Lake Brienz.

Several villages line the course, and enthusiastic local crowds cheer along the entire route (you'll hear a lot of cowbells, as well as alpenhorn players). At the halfway point, you're treated to a lovely view of Staubbach Falls, the highest waterfall in Switzerland. Keep that serenity in mind as you hit the second half of the course, where one of the most difficult challenges in distance running lies in wait. Around the 26K mark, almost every participant will be slowed to a walk by a steep ascent named The Wall. Over this 5K stretch, runners will climb 1,568 feet (478 m). Once you clear The Wall, you're well on your way to the finish line in Eigergletscher, 7,600 feet (2,316 m) above sea level. Luckily, you are not required to run back down the mountain!

Once you're at the top, you've finished the race! Lots of refreshments are available at the finish line, as well as hot showers—so pack a change of clothes. After you freshen up, the race rewards you further with a stunning cable car ride down the mountain, plus a scenic train back to Interlaken.

Jungfrau has intimidating elevation gain, but its views offer incredible rewards for the challenge.

LOST LAKE RUN

A classic backcountry Alaska experience

SEASON: **Summer**   TOTAL NO. OF RUNNERS: **750**   RACE DISTANCE: **16 miles (26 km)**
ELEVATION GAIN: **2,600 feet (792 m)**   DIFFICULTY: **Moderate**

The Lost Lake Run has become so popular, it often sells out within minutes of opening registration. No wonder—the Alaska wilderness is an absolute paradise. The race takes place in Kenai Fjords National Park, which encompasses the outflowing glaciers of the Harding Icefield, as well as coastal fjords, islands, and the Kenai Peninsula. The first five miles (8 km) are uphill and represent the bulk of the elevation gain on the course. The grind to the top will be worth it once you're on the ridge above the tree line. On a clear day, you're rewarded with awe-inspiring views of the Chugach Mountains, the town of Seward, and broad swaths of the national park. The trails in Kenai Fjords are smooth and runnable, and as the race pack thins out, you may catch some wildlife sightings. The area is known for its black bears, so keep your eyes peeled, though don't worry: They aren't known to bother speedy trail runners.

Founded in 1992 as a fundraiser, the race still keeps the cause central. Runners collect pledges for the fight to cure cystic fibrosis, and since the race's inception, more than $2 million has been donated to the Cystic Fibrosis Foundation.

Visiting Seward is well worth the trip, too, with so much lush wilderness to explore. But if you want to give your legs a rest postrace, you can enjoy a day cruise of Resurrection Bay to catch sightings of marine wildlife and dramatic mountain views. You might also enjoy a day of chartered fishing for halibut or salmon. Eating fresh fish after a big run is a nutritious and delectable way to recover.

Let the finish-line barbecue be motivation as you navigate various river crossings.

ULTRA-TRAIL DU MONT-BLANC

The mythical pinnacle of ultrarunning

SEASON: Summer   **TOTAL NO. OF RUNNERS:** 2,600   **RACE DISTANCE:** 106 miles (171 km)
ELEVATION GAIN: 32,687 feet (9,963 m)   **DIFFICULTY:** Challenging

Any race that touches three different countries is going to be epic. The Ultra-Trail du Mont-Blanc (UTMB) circumnavigates the titular Alpine peak through portions of France, Italy, and Switzerland, and that enticing hook has made this one of the preeminent events in ultrarunning. Each year, fans and spectators from around the world are glued to the live stream for a full 24 hours. That's because it takes the fastest runners about 19 hours to complete the course and return to Chamonix, home of both the start and finish lines. The back of the pack might take as long as 48 hours to complete the race.

For runners and travelers, the scene in Chamonix during race week is that of a trail-running Super Bowl. The small Alpine village is mobbed with participants, corporate sponsors, media, and fans. The days leading up to the ultra feature six other race distances, encapsulating a total of 10,000 competitors. By Friday night, when UTMB begins, the excitement is at a fever pitch. The instrumental notes of "Conquest of Paradise" resound through the streets, and spectators pack the starting line. It will bring chills to any fan—and participant.

In between the feel-good moments of the start and finish are 106 miles of mountain terrain, with a jaw-dropping 32,687 feet (9,963 m) of climbing in and out of mountain villages along the course. (For those there to cheer on

OPPOSITE: The race begins in Chamonix at the base of Mont Blanc.

PAGES 290–291: Race organizers refer to this ultra as an "introspective adventure." You'll know what they mean as you trek along rocky cliffsides.

or otherwise support runners at various aid stations, buses ferry you along the route so you don't have to navigate driving in three countries.) The Alps provide plenty of all-natural beauty for the thrill seekers taking on the course: When racers aren't running through the night or fighting severe fatigue, their eyes are feasting on endless peaks, glaciers, pine forests, wildflower-dotted valleys, pastures, and lakes.

The grueling route is for only the most experienced ultrarunners, and entry standards are in place to ensure that nonprofessional athletes are qualified to toe the line. Though the requirements change from year to year, they often involve finishing select races within a certain time frame. If running UTMB is your goal, plan a couple years ahead so you can run a qualifying race first, then register for the big one.

Even if racing isn't in the cards for you, those who appreciate running or hiking in the Alps can traverse the Ultra-Trail du Mont-Blanc course on their own. Although the tour is still challenging and requires preparation, slowing down and drinking in the views will be just as rewarding and fun.

TRAVEL TIP

There's plenty of buzz and excitement in Chamonix in the days leading up to the race. You'll see your favorite elite athletes, brands throwing parties or hosting group runs, and runners finishing other race distances at all hours. If you'd like a quieter place to rest, consider staying in any of the nearby towns and villages outside Chamonix.

PIKES PEAK MARATHON AND ASCENT

One of Colorado's famous 14ers

**SEASON: Fall   TOTAL NO. OF RUNNERS: 2,000   RACE DISTANCES: 13.3-mile (21.4 km) Ascent; marathon
ELEVATION GAIN: 7,800 feet (2,377 m)   DIFFICULTY: Challenging**

Colorado boasts 58 named mountain peaks higher than 14,000 feet (4,267 m) above sea level. One such mountain is Pikes Peak, which has held a race to the top every year since 1956. So the Pikes Peak Marathon and Ascent feature a long history of runners who have put themselves to the ultimate test.

The course begins in Manitou Springs, a town just outside Colorado Springs. Runners have two options for racing: On Saturday, the Ascent is a 13.3-mile run to the top, where shuttle buses wait to take everybody back down the mountain. On Sunday, the Pikes Peak Marathon requires runners to climb the peak again, then descend into Manitou Springs by foot, where the race finishes.

In both races, the course uses the narrow and steep Barr Trail, which has an average grade of 11 percent. Breaking down the course into segments helps you keep moving forward. The first milestone is Barr Camp, at mile 7.6. Volunteers arrive at this aid station on Friday night and spend the whole weekend pumping water by hand through a filter station to pass out on race days. Don't forget to thank them!

About three miles (4.8 km) from the summit (mile 10), you'll see an A-frame shelter marking a difficult section of the course. This section has more than 2,000 feet (610 m) of elevation gain and a grade upwards of 12 percent. Even

TRAVEL TIP

Manitou Springs, your home base for the weekend, is 6,412 feet (1,954 m) above sea level—obviously, you'll go even higher on race day. So unless you're arriving weeks ahead of time, your body will not have time to acclimate. Hydrate *a lot*, and adjust your pace and expectations.

OPPOSITE: The average grade awaiting runners starting at Manitou Springs measures 11 percent.

PAGES 294-295: Manitou Springs offers plenty to tour, including Indigenous cliff dwellings and Victorian Miramont Castle.

the fastest runners resort to hiking here. Remember: The higher you go, the more you need to fuel your body. Take in calories and stay hydrated. Bring snacks and your own hydration system to supplement the aid stations.

Next, look for the "16 Golden Stairs," the 32 switchbacks that lead to the summit. This part of the route is notoriously rocky, with step-ups that feel high at this stage of the game. You're in the homestretch, so even if you're tapped, focus on putting one foot in front of the other.

Sunday's marathon course comes back down the same trail. That means faster runners will cross paths with slower runners. As a courtesy and for safety, keep your eyes up and know that some elite athletes may bomb down the trail, which is narrow. Downhill runners have the right-of-way, so scoot to the inside and give them space to pass when it's safe to do so.

At the top of Pikes Peak, take in the landscape. On a clear day you can see six states: Colorado, New Mexico, Kansas, Nebraska, Wyoming, and

APRÈS RACE

You're not far from Colorado Springs, a hot spot for outdoor recreation and more. If you can extend your trip, explore what the area has to offer, including the Garden of the Gods park, the Rocky Mountain Motorcycle Museum, white-water rafting the Arkansas River, or driving Skyline Drive, a scenic, roller coaster–like route along the mountains with views into Cañon City.

ABOVE: Swiss runner Rémi Bonnet breaks the Ascent record in 2023.

OPPOSITE: The 2023 race's female champion, American Sophia Laukli (right), embraces runner-up Judith Wyder, from Switzerland, at the finish.

Oklahoma. You might even notice the curvature of Earth fading into the distance. You've really climbed *that* high.

When it's time to run back to Manitou Springs, watch your footing and enjoy the gravitational pull (watch out for a few unexpected "ups" on the way down). Be careful, but be encouraged by the notion that stumbles seem to be part of the fun. Everyone at the finish line has a story to tell, and the scrapes and bruises to go with it.

Manitou Springs becomes a runners' block party in the aftermath of the race, so stick around and enjoy the festive atmosphere. The town has plenty of restaurants to choose from, and you can hit one of Manitou's eight mineral hot springs, thought to have healing powers, to soothe your aching muscles. After scaling a mountain, it certainly couldn't hurt to try.

TWO OCEANS MARATHON

South Africa's best loved road race, with an intense cutoff time

SEASON: Southern Hemisphere fall   **NO. OF MARATHON RUNNERS:** 13,000   **RACE DISTANCES:** Half-marathon; marathon; 56K (34.8 mi)   **ELEVATION GAIN:** 2,077 feet (633 m)   **DIFFICULTY:** Moderate

The Two Oceans Marathon is so named because the course around the Cape Horn Peninsula takes in both the Indian and Atlantic Oceans. It's among the most popular races in the country and attracts runners from around the world, too, not just for the spectacular scenery but also for the warmth and hospitality of the locals. Truly, nobody cares less about your finishing time and more about your race-day experience than South Africans (although, if you're close to the race's cutoff time, they might motivate you to pick up the pace and reach the finish!).

The event takes place over Easter weekend and is central to a celebratory festival, with 13,000 people in the ultra and a whopping 16,000 people taking part in the half-marathon.

The first 19 miles (30 km) are mostly flat, but don't let the easy terrain lure you into running faster than you should. The most dramatic part of the course is the climb up Chapman's Peak around mile 20, where sheer cliffs drop off right into the Atlantic below. Take a moment to relish that sight. Another climb is ahead, around mile 28 up Constantia Nek. The finish line is always a dramatic scene, as the seven-hour cutoff time is strictly enforced. After seven hours, a gun goes off and the line is roped off immediately. That won't stop spectators from willing dogged runners near the back to pour it on during the final countdown.

After Chapman's Peak, runners will be treated with a gorgeous view of Hout Bay.

WESTERN STATES ENDURANCE RUN

The world's oldest 100-mile trail race has lasted this long for a reason.

SEASON: Summer   **TOTAL NO. OF RUNNERS: 380**   **RACE DISTANCE: 100 miles (160.9 km)**
ELEVATION GAIN: 18,000 feet (5,486 m)   **DIFFICULTY: Challenging**

As the runners take off in the early morning hours from California's Olympic Valley, a stream of headlamps light the way up to Emigrant Pass, climbing 2,550 feet (777 m) in the first 4.5 miles (7.2 km) of this special 100-mile race. It's a grueling way to kick off one of running's most challenging endurance tests, but the timing is intentional. As racers crest Emigrant Pass, the sun should be rising just behind them—a gorgeous moment that only adds to the adventure ahead.

The Western States Endurance Run, which has been around since 1977, is a favorite among ultrarunners. The story goes that in 1974, ultrarunning legend Gordy Ainsleigh joined the Western States Trail Ride—a horse ride—to see if he could complete the course on foot. He made it to the finish line in Auburn, California, in 24 hours 42 minutes. And thus, the 100-mile trail run was born.

The course is no walk in the park. Temperatures fluctuate from chilly in the morning to scorching hot (100°F/37.7°C or more sometimes) in the afternoon, as participants traverse the canyons. The Western States Trail itself extends from Salt Lake City, Utah, to Sacramento, California, and the race follows the middle portion from Olympic Valley westward, to Auburn, ending on the Placer High School track. The terrain is remote and comes with some arduous climbs, including one up Deadwood Canyon that rises

RACE DAY TIP

Ultras like Western States allow you to have a crew and pacers for support. These team members give you whatever you need—fresh clothes, a restock of on-course snacks, hydration vest refills, and hugs—at aid stations. Pacers can run alongside you for portions to lend encouragement and company.

OPPOSITE: Mile 78 features the infamous American River crossing. A guide rope helps runners across.

PAGES 302-303: Prepare for extremes! Temperatures can vary widely on the run.

1,800 feet (550 m), and 36 switchbacks to the Devil's Thumb aid station at mile 47. Then it's another plunge into El Dorado Canyon, which means you'll have to climb out of that one too. You pop up in Michigan Bluff, an old mining town, and you've got one more canyon after that—Volcano Canyon. This one ends up at mile 62, in Forest Hills—the rowdiest aid station on the course, and exactly when you need encouragement most.

Just before landing at the Green Gate aid station, you'll cross the American River at mile 78. This is a great opportunity to cool off—many runners dunk their heads—but be careful, as it's easy to slip here. A guide rope will lead you across, manned by volunteers in life vests to keep you upright, and in high-water years, more volunteers will give you a lift in a river raft instead.

After exiting the river, you have another two-mile (3.2 km) climb to the next aid station at mile 80. For most humans, 20 more miles (32 km) of running would seem like a lot. For an ultrarunner conquering a 100-miler? It's the homestretch. After passing No Hands Bridge at the confluence

TRAVEL TIP

Most runners stay in Olympic Valley in the days leading up to Western States. It's a peaceful setting in the mountains but an exciting atmosphere on race weekend. Because the course is point-to-point, however, you likely won't want to drive back after you finish. Book a hotel close to Auburn for after the run and have your crew bring your luggage. You'll be happy to have a hot shower and bed so close.

of the North and Middle Forks of the American River, you're in the *real* home-stretch—mile 96.5. Soon you find yourself on paved roads in the town of Auburn with just 1.3 miles (2.1 km) left. Never mind that steep climb to the "Mile 99" sign. You'll see lights illuminating the track and hear fans ready to greet you. Just 250 meters around the oval and you're a Western States finisher.

One of the more endearing parts of Western States is what's known as the Golden Hour. At this time, the Placer High School track fills with runners who have finished, as well as spectators, volunteers, and fans to cheer on runners finishing in the final hour before the cutoff time. Every year, the race officially ends at 10:59:59 a.m. on Sunday, and every year, there are participants on the cusp of making it in time. Those who reach the track with mere minutes to spare will have the undying support of the entire race community as they scream for those final steps—it's one of the most heartwarming scenes in all of running.

PART FOUR

RUNS, NOT RACES

A boardwalk supports runners across a tussock field along the epic Pouākai Circuit (page 320) in New Zealand's Egmont National Park.

KALALAU TRAIL

A secret passage to the Nā Pali Coast

BEST TIME TO GO: Mid-May to early October   **WHAT YOU'LL SEE:** Waterfalls, jungle cliffs
DISTANCE: 22 miles (35 km) out and back   **DIFFICULTY:** Challenging

Most people only see the Nā Pali Coast, on the northwest side of Kauai, by sea or helicopter. Runners, of course, are not most people. The Kalalau Trail, which begins in Ke'e Beach, is a gorgeous hiking or running tour of this spectacular area. This magical trek takes you by cascading waterfalls and in view of the sparkling Pacific Ocean from high atop exposed ridges.

The route holds historical significance for the Indigenous people of Hawaii, though the trail today is not the same as it was centuries ago. Ancient Hawaiians used similar footpaths to connect and trade with communities across the different valleys along the coast. Be mindful of this history and respect the trails.

Most runners and hikers break the trail into segments. The first two miles (3.2 km) of the trail will probably be crowded with non-permit-holding day hikers. You'll need a permit to go the distance. In the spring of 2018, floods and landslides damaged the route, which took a year to repair. To preserve the trail, the state's Department of Land and Natural Resources instituted the permit process to limit access. Fortunately, acquiring a permit is relatively easy if you plan ahead; it just takes a visit to the trail website.

Along the route, you'll encounter Hanakapi'ai Stream, a common stopping point if the water level is high. Pay attention to local advisories, and

OPPOSITE: Jade ridges loom majestically over Kalalau Beach.

PAGES 310-311: While most take in the Nā Pali Coast from the air, a run along the cliffs offers an intimate sunset view.

don't attempt to ford if advised otherwise, or if the water is fast or high (people have died amid ill-advised crossing attempts). In general, the route has some precarious technical aspects, including narrow cliffside single-tracks, multiple stream crossings, and slick or muddy conditions. Don't push yourself—or your group—beyond comfort zones.

You may be on the coastline, but that doesn't mean this trail is flat. In fact, it's quite hilly, and there's some decent climbing involved. After the Hanakapi'ai Stream crossing, the route goes inland and the scenery is more jungle than beach (translation: muddy). Mile six (9.7 km) is a good time to check in with yourself and make sure you're up for continuing to the turnaround point at Kalalau Beach. The second half of the trail, though typically drier than the first half, is demanding and includes the infamous "Crawler's Ledge." This is not meant for anybody who is scared of heights. A 20-foot (6.1 m) section on the razor's edge of the cliff drops straight into the Pacific Ocean. This is where the run of a lifetime is more like a deliberate, careful hike of a lifetime.

GEAR CHECK

Although road running shoes work fine on many trails, you may have better traction if you wear trail shoes on Kalalau. Invest in a pair that mimics the feel of your road shoes but has grippy tread on the soles.

Your reward for navigating the tricky back half of the trail is a respite on Kalalau Beach, a one-mile (1.6 km) stretch of sandy shoreline, bound by lush forest. Here, you can catch your breath, gather your strength, enjoy the tranquility, and maybe explore a few sea coves before you head back in the direction you came. Recovery on the beach can be sublime: Soak your legs in the ocean and cool off underneath the waterfall. You'll feel refreshed and ready to get back on your feet to conquer Crawler's Ledge one more time.

TRAVEL TIP

Although it will make your outing more of a backpacking hike than a run, your permit allows up to five nights of camping at Kalalau Beach. You could use the area as a home base to run parts of the trail while you're there—and extend your stay in a remote paradise.

ABOVE: **Red Hill leads you on a sharp descent to Kalalau Beach.**

OPPOSITE: **The most popular hiking trail is the two-mile (3.2 km) stretch from Ke'e Beach to Hanakapi'ai Valley, but venturing two more miles will take you to Hanakapi'ai Falls.**

CHESAPEAKE & OHIO CANAL TOWPATH

A repurposed running retreat hidden in urban sprawl

BEST TIME TO GO: Year-round
DISTANCE: 184 miles (296 km)

WHAT YOU'LL SEE: Great blue herons, songbirds, ducks
DIFFICULTY: Easy

The C&O Canal Towpath is a lifeline to runners living in Washington, D.C., and the greater metro area. The dirt and stone path begins in Georgetown and extends northwest to Cumberland, Maryland. It's a flat, traffic-free oasis full of runners, walkers, and cyclists. The towpath was originally built for the canal mules that towed boats through the waterway. The canal, however, was kind of a bust. By the time it was completed in 1850, railroads had already taken over as the primary shipping method. To boot, a flood destroyed the whole operation in 1924.

Today, Chesapeake & Ohio Canal National Historical Park, through which the trail runs, is a 20,000-acre (8,094 ha) recreational corridor. Many sections of the trail are under canopies of trees that provide shade during the muggy summer and vibrant colors in fall. You can pick up the path in Georgetown on 29th Street NW, south of M Street.

The towpath makes a great complement to an already active Washington metropolitan area vacation. It's ideal for race shakeout runs in and around D.C. too. If you really want to make the towpath an adventure, rent one of the historic lockhouses. In the early 1900s, the lockkeepers who opened and closed the canal gates for boats slept here during their shifts. Today, many of the houses, including some that are period-preserved—meaning no air-conditioning, electricity, or running water—can be rented out.

The C&O Canal Towpath takes runners through historic Georgetown.

CENTRAL PARK

An iconic run in the world's most famous green space

BEST TIME TO GO: **Year-round**   WHAT YOU'LL SEE: **Belvedere Castle, the Met, Bethesda Terrace, and more**
DISTANCE: **6 miles (9.7 km)**   DIFFICULTY: **Easy**

You'll find runners circling Central Park in the heart of Manhattan at all hours of the day and night. The longest loop around this urban gem is six miles of paved road, but you can go as far as you want with endless combinations of routes through the 843-acre (341 ha) urban green space.

Enter the park almost anywhere from Central Park South to 110th Street and you'll pick up the Park Drive running path. You'll find some rolling hills in almost any direction, but they're not challenging enough to cause alarm—they really just keep things interesting.

For softer surfaces, head to the reservoir. The southern edge of the reservoir is around 86th Street. A crushed gravel path surrounds the body of water. You can circle the mostly flat 1.6-mile (2.5 km) loop and take in the views of Midtown Manhattan from there—it's best in the morning, before the congestion of the day. Alternatively, stay on the gravel and dirt bridle path beneath the reservoir for a 1.7-mile (2.7 km) loop. The bridle path extends 4.2 miles (6.8 km) when you add its sections north and south of the reservoir on the west side. This route is a nice way to get off the concrete and see some of the nooks and crannies of Central Park that you'd miss on the roads, including expansive meadows, classical bridges such as the Bow Bridge, and possibly horseback riders.

RUNNING TIP

If you're not staying near Central Park, or want to go for a run in the middle of a long day in Manhattan, the New York Road Runners Run Center on West 57th Street offers lockers with electronic locks to store your belongings, charging stations for your phone and other devices, plus ample space to stretch, rest, and rehydrate.

OPPOSITE: An evening run can offer a respite from the rush hour bustle of the city.

PAGES 318-319: You'll spot numerous running groups in the park, including the Upper West Side Run Club.

For those who want to stick to the roads, the Park Drive loop circumnavigates the whole park. The road can be crowded with other runners, walkers, cyclists, horse carriages, and tourists navigating the park for the first time, so pay attention to your surroundings. Cut across 72nd Street to visit Bethesda Terrace overlooking the Ramble and Lake woodland area (designed to look like the forests of upstate New York). People-watch and relax by Bethesda Fountain.

From Bethesda Terrace, continue to the west side and head south on the Park Drive. Soon you'll see the Tavern on the Green (the park's iconic restaurant) on your right and Sheep Meadow on your left. You've arrived at the famed finish of the New York City Marathon (though you're approaching from the opposite direction that you would on race day). Take a moment to imagine what it's like on the first Sunday of November as 50,000 runners pass over that line, completing their journey from Staten Island. Though Central Park is a runner's refuge all year long, its splendor can be fully appreciated in the fall, when the trees are ablaze in yellows, reds, and oranges against the backdrop of the city skyline.

And if you ever find yourself lost in the park, every light pole has the closest street location stamped at its base. The first two digits represent the street, and the final two digits indicate which side of the park you're in—even numbers are east, odd are west.

POUĀKAI CIRCUIT

Circle a volcano while running through morphing wetlands.

BEST TIME TO GO: October to April **WHAT YOU'LL SEE:** Mount Taranaki **DISTANCE:** 16.2 miles (26 km)
DIFFICULTY: Challenging

The Pouākai Circuit (or Circuit Track as it's known locally) is a demanding route in Egmont National Park, on the west coast of the North Island. It features essential views of Mount Taranaki, a dormant stratovolcano rising 8,000 feet (2,438 m) above sea level. And if that's not enough adventure for you, a round-trip trail to the top of the volcano stretches another eight miles (12.9 km).

The Pouākai Circuit is a daylong excursion for most runners, due to the diversity of terrain and plentiful climbing throughout the trek. A lot of the track is runnable, but sections of volcanic rock will require hiking instead. You'll encounter forestland, alpine tussock fields thick with grass, lakes, and swampland. You'll also see highlights like the Boomerang Slip, a volcanic scar on the landscape formed by a landslide (watch your step on the loose scree), and the Dieffenbach Cliffs. The Ahukawakawa Swamp, an alpine wetland packed with unique flora, requires runners to cross a boardwalk. Climbing out of the swamp requires navigating some steps and stairs.

For those who would rather slow down and break this run up into two days, the route has huts that welcome hikers. You can reserve a bunk online if you'd rather not leave it to chance. With such a diverse landscape, this is an excellent route for those who prefer to have a wide variety of scenery.

The boardwalk offers protection through the swampland, but water and mud overtake the trail in places. Wear trail shoes!

CONUNDRUM CREEK TRAIL

A soothing soak awaits you at the top of this trail run.

BEST TIME TO GO: July to September   **WHAT YOU'LL SEE:** Wildflowers, snowy mountain peaks
DISTANCE: 17 miles (27 km)   **DIFFICULTY:** Challenging

The Conundrum Creek Trail in Aspen, Colorado, culminates with a high-altitude hot spring, certain bliss to any endurance athlete. Of course, the catch is you have to endure an 8.5-mile (13.7 km) run up a mountain and about 2,400 feet (732 m) of elevation gain to reach it. The trailhead begins at 8,700 feet (2,652 m) and the route tops out at 11,200 feet (3,414 m), so those who seek the spring should be prepared for unpredictable mountain weather (it's not unusual to see snowpack, even in the summer). Luckily, the incline is more gradual than steep, and the trail winds through beautiful aspen groves, pine forests, and green meadows before releasing you above the tree line. In summer, you're bound to feel awestruck by the plethora of multicolored wildflowers. In fall, aspens turn golden, one of the signature sights amid the Maroon Bells–Snowmass Wilderness.

As the hot spring becomes more well known, it's best to get an early start on the trail if you don't want to share the pool with a crowd of strangers. Experienced trail runners can tackle the climb and descent in one day, but those less willing to leg it out might consider camping overnight—you'll need a permit to do so. If you do try the whole enchilada in one day, bring an extra pair of shoes or socks for the drive home: You'll have three creek crossings each way on the trail—one of them requires wading through the water and the other two have primitive log bridges.

Does post-run (or mid-run) recovery get any better than a soak in natural hot springs?

DEATH VALLEY NATIONAL PARK

Welcome to the land of extremes.

BEST TIME TO GO: Death Valley **WHAT YOU'LL SEE:** Sand dunes, salt mounds, canyons, basins
DISTANCE: Variable   **DIFFICULTY:** Moderate to challenging

The hottest, driest, and lowest national park in the United States offers runners a vast array—3.4 million acres (1.3 million ha)—of terrain to choose from when they commit to these trails. And it's not all barren sands and rocky crags. From the highest point in the park, Telescope Peak, 11,049 feet (3,368 m) above sea level, to Badwater Basin, 282 feet (86 m) below sea level, the difference between the extremes of Death Valley is twice the depth of the Grand Canyon.

The sheer vastness of Death Valley can be overwhelming for visitors, and that's especially true for runners looking for the best routes during their stay. Maximize your options by planning a stay in the winter or early spring. Death Valley is prohibitively, dangerously hot in the summer, with average July temperatures at 116°F (46.6°C). Winters, meanwhile, are downright perfect for runners: January sees average highs of 67°F (19.4°C) and lows near 40°F (4.4°C).

Plan your runs according to the park's features—each offers a different kind of day. The Mesquite Flat Sand Dunes are a free-for-all—with no trails to follow, you can just choose your own adventure. Badwater Basin, meanwhile, is the starting point of the famous Badwater 135 Ultramarathon, which is held in July. While that race stretches to Mount Whitney, stay in the basin to challenge yourself on its uneven, ever changing salt flats.

OPPOSITE: Weather near the Ubehebe Crater can be brisk in winter. Bring long sleeves just in case.

PAGES 326-327: For a challenging training run, the Mesquite Flat Sand Dunes provide plenty of resistance.

Death Valley also offers plenty of places to log vertical miles too. Dante's View is a perfect spot to watch the sunset over the valley below. It's about 15 miles (24 km) from the Furnace Creek Visitor Center, and the run to the top is just under six miles (9.7 km). Another option is the Telescope Peak Trail, about 14 miles (22.5 km) round trip (bring layers in the wintertime—the mountainous terrain can reach near freezing temperatures).

If you're a lucky springtime traveler, Death Valley will treat you to some of the loveliest displays of wildflowers you've ever seen. The bloom depends on the fall and winter rainfall, a lack of drying winds, and sufficient warmth, which can be difficult—if not impossible—to predict. But when all things align, it leads to spectacular fields of desert gold, with mariposa lilies, bear poppies, desert chicories, and more.

RUNNING TIP

Heed park officials' advice. Rangers at Death Valley advise against running in the summer months. Even if you run in late spring, take precautions. Go as early as possible in the day, hydrate like a racehorse, and wear protective clothing, including headwear and eyewear.

WAITUKUBULI NATIONAL TRAIL

A rugged trek to some of the Caribbean's most beautiful locales

BEST TIME TO GO: December to May   **WHAT YOU'LL SEE:** Rainforests, gorges, waterfalls
DISTANCE: 115 miles (185 km)   **DIFFICULTY:** Challenging

Dominica is known as Nature Island of the Caribbean because of its rugged and mostly untouched wilderness. As the youngest island in the Lesser Antilles, it's actually still evolving, thanks to geothermal volcanic activity. The official language on the island is English, but the country has a French Creole culture, influenced by the neighboring islands of Guadeloupe and Martinique. With a unique interior landscape to go with beautiful beaches, this isn't your typical Caribbean getaway.

The Waitukubuli National Trail covers almost all the territory of Dominica. The mountainous rainforests, which cover 60 percent of the island, are among the most rain-soaked land in the world. Which is to say, you'll encounter a lot of mud. Hikers break the trail down into 14 different segments, often according to terrain, and trail runners can choose which segments suit their desires or abilities. You'll find coastal views, elfin forests, volcanic territory, deep gorges, and natural hot springs along Waitukubuli, as well as Morne Diablotins, Dominica's highest peak, at 4,747 feet (1,447 m). There's also an 8.1-mile (13 km) trail to the famous Boiling Lake, the second largest hot lake in the world. It's not a swimming hole, though—the water temperature sits at about 197°F (92°C) on the *edges*. Don't attempt to jump in, or even touch, the water.

The trail starts at Scott's Head on the southern end of the island, or at Cabrits National Park on the northern end.

Proximity to the ocean helps this trail integrate into any travel plans, from relaxing on the sand to an afternoon scuba dive.

THREE PASSES TREK

A daring journey in view of the world's most famous peak, for expert trail runners only

BEST TIME TO GO: Fall or spring   **WHAT YOU'LL SEE: Mount Everest**   **DISTANCE: 103 miles (166 km)**
DIFFICULTY: Challenging

For those seeking an intense altitude challenge, the Khumbu Valley in Nepal is a dream come true. Traversing the Three Passes—Renjo La (17,513 feet/5,388 m), Cho La (17,650 feet/5,380 m), and Kongma La (18,159 feet/5,535 m)—isn't for the faint of heart, but the supportive and experienced people of Nepal will guide your way.

This once-in-a-lifetime experience requires a lot of logistics. Visitors fly into Kathmandu, then choose to start the journey either from Jiri, which adds mileage, or from Lukla, which requires another flight into the airport known as the most dangerous in the world because of its short runway and fast landings in very thin air. Don't fret: Lukla is also the gateway to Mount Everest, so people fly in and out of it every day without incident.

Wherever you start and end your adventure, and whether you decide to go clockwise or counterclockwise on the trail, the Three Passes require plenty of training and preparation. Give yourself at least six months, if not a year, to build the strength and stamina required to traverse the highest summits in the world, and extra time within your trip to account for planned and unplanned rest days. Even the fittest athletes are never sure how their bodies will adapt to the extreme altitude. Under these conditions, you never want to be in a hurry.

The most popular accommodations along the Three Passes Trek are teahouses, where you'll typically sleep in a simple room and share a bathroom with other guests. Some teahouses have hot showers for an extra charge,

TRAVEL TIP

High altitude is taxing on the body. Many runners pad their time in Nepal to acclimate to the extreme conditions. Heed the signs of altitude sickness: headache, vomiting, dizziness, vision changes, and other uncomfortable symptoms. Rest, hydrate, and, if conditions grow severe, descend to lower altitude as quickly as possible.

OPPOSITE: Everest towers over Namche Bazaar, the main hub where you can gather supplies and prep for your trek.

PAGES 332-333: These climbers are about to summit Kala Patthar to view the sunrise over Everest.

but you can use cold water for free. Charging electronics might also be an additional cost. The teahouses usually serve local fare like *dal bhat* (rice, vegetables, and lentils). A guide can be useful for navigating the intricacies of local accommodations and customs, as well as local laws concerning safety on the trails.

The Kongma La is the highest and easternmost pass, and many runners start their trip there under the assumption they'll have more energy at the beginning. This route is also the longest stretch between villages where you'll likely stay—Chukhung to the east and Lobuche to the west. You'll cross the Khumbu Glacier, marked by cairns so you won't get lost.

The second pass, whichever direction you're going, is Cho La, which connects the popular valleys that include Everest Base Camp and Gokyo Lakes (if you want to see Everest Base Camp, you can extend your stay to include it). This is considered the most technical of the terrain because you may encounter snow or ice on the Cho La Glacier. Some runners feel more comfortable if they utilize shoe traction such as MICROspikes. The nearest villages are Dzongla (east) and Dragnag (west).

Renjo La is the lowest of the three passes, between Gokyo and Lumde. The trail offers stellar views of Everest and other Himalayan peaks, as well as glimpses of the Gokyo Lakes and Ngozumpa Glacier, the longest glacier in the region.

THE FOREST OF NISENE MARKS STATE PARK

A path through a revitalized forest with a climactic waterfall

BEST TIME TO GO: Year-round   **WHAT YOU'LL SEE:** Redwood tree groves, deer, occasional mountain lion
DISTANCE: Variable; 30 miles (48 km) of trails   **DIFFICULTY:** Moderate

When you arrive at The Forest of Nisene Marks State Park, you'll have a hard time imagining that it had been clear-cut in the 1900s during a logging frenzy. Mother Nature has done a lot of work to regrow this beautiful landscape, thanks in part to support from the family of Nisene Marks, a local nature lover whose children donated 9,700 acres (3,925 ha) to the state of California in 1963. Today, the park is protected land and has expanded to 10,000 acres (4,047 ha), offering 30 miles of trails to run.

A favorite local route is Sand Point, which is 13 miles (21 km) long and offers 2,000 feet (610 m) of elevation gain. On this trail, you'll experience a large portion of the state park. Aptos Creek Fire Road—a gravel road that rises to Sand Point—features heavily into many of the most popular adventures. If it's a clear day, you might catch a glimpse of the Pacific Ocean up there. Follow the single-track West Ridge Trail to complete the loop.

One of the most popular treks for tourists includes visiting the epicenter of the magnitude 6.9 Loma Prieta earthquake, which struck on October 17, 1989. The quake lasted 15 seconds, killing 63 people. Its epicenter was traced

OPPOSITE: One of the popular trails in the park is Maple Falls, a 9.9-mile (15.9 km) out-and-back.

PAGES 336-337: The park stretches from sea level to coastal mountains, with plenty of greenery to see along the way.

to the park in a spot along Aptos Creek, which you can find by running the Aptos Creek Trail, about a six-mile (9.7 km), round-trip jaunt. The spot is marked with a simple sign, after two stream crossings.

Maple Falls offers a fantastically varied and exhilarating run for another long day. It's about 10 miles (16.1 km) round trip and offers a few creek crossings, canyon views, and lush fern-lined pathways. It all leads to a waterfall cascading underneath a canopy of maples.

California's Central Coast offers plenty of busy beach towns to turn a visit to The Forest of Nisene Marks into a road trip. Santa Cruz makes for a great stop. Nisene Marks offers picnic areas aplenty and ample shade if you're looking for a rest on a long, active day.

RUNNING TIP

The Forest of Nisene Marks is the perfect place for bird-watching runners to combine their two favorite hobbies. The area is filled with unique and marvelous species, including pileated woodpeckers, marbled murrelets, and various hawks.

PYRAMIDS OF GIZA

Quite simply, the most epic run

BEST TIME TO GO: October to May   **WHAT YOU'LL SEE:** The Sahara, Great Pyramid of Giza, Great Sphinx
DISTANCE: Variable   **DIFFICULTY:** Easy

Cairo is a popular destination for travelers to Egypt, but busy streets, heavy traffic, and air quality can make it difficult for runners to carve out a path for training. Endurance athletes shouldn't be deterred, however, from visiting this historic and energetic Egyptian capital. An unforgettable run waits just 12 miles (19 km) outside the city: the dunes and lesser-traveled roads surrounding the Pyramids at Giza and the Great Sphinx.

The Great Sphinx of Giza, a limestone statue of a lion with a human head, measures 240 feet (73 m) long and 66 feet (20 m) high. Historians estimate it was built around 2500 B.C., perhaps as a monument to the pharaoh Khafre. The Great Pyramid, meanwhile, was built about 100 years earlier as the tomb of the pharaoh Khufu.

You're here for the scenery, not necessarily the miles. The area is small, but you can make a worthy run out of traversing the sand dunes—just keep the pyramid within your sight line, as the otherwise featureless desert can make it easy to become disoriented. The surrounding roads also offer focus and informal checkpoints. And though you may be tempted to run up to these epic monoliths, please don't. It's illegal to climb these or any of the other pyramids at this UNESCO World Heritage site. The pyramids are open from 8 a.m. to 5 p.m. every day, and crowds are lightest earlier in the morning.

A run in view of the Pyramids at Giza and the Great Sphinx—how epic is that?

HALEAKALĀ NATIONAL PARK

A steep climb out of a painterly landscape

BEST TIME TO GO: Fall   **WHAT YOU'LL SEE: Bamboo forests, volcanic craters, waterfalls**
DISTANCE: Variable   **DIFFICULTY: Challenging**

Haleakalā National Park is divided into two districts, each with a unique landscape and dense forest. The Summit District features the eponymous dormant volcano and a massive valley. The Coastal District is marked by bamboo forests and striking waterfalls. Both are worth visiting, depending on what kind of run you're looking for, and offer a diversity of trail experiences.

The Sliding Sands Trail in the Summit District is an iconic favorite. This demanding trek descends into the valley—or crater—along an 11-mile (17.7 km) trail that actually starts at the summit of Haleakalā volcano. At 10,023 feet (3,055 m) above sea level, remember that you'll have to climb back up to the summit for the second half of this run, so measure your effort accordingly (don't discount the sandy footing—it adds to the challenge). Around 5.5 miles (8.9 km), you'll pass Pele's Paint Pot. Here, the oxidized volcanic minerals make the surface appear as if a painter brushed the landscape in strokes of red, orange, yellow, and white. You'll also encounter silverswords, flowering perennial plants that are now a protected species.

Haleakalā is a sacred area for Hawaiians, so respect your surroundings and strictly stick to the trails. Make sure to pack warm clothes while visiting this area. Surprisingly for Maui, temperatures in Haleakalā National Park can dip below freezing at the top of the volcano. Layers are advised.

Unless you want your luggage smelling like a volcano, bring a spare laundry bag to keep your run gear separate.

FLORIDA KEYS OVERSEAS HERITAGE TRAIL

Where you can travel from key to key, entirely on foot

BEST TIME TO GO: December to March   **WHAT YOU'LL SEE:** Great white egrets, terns, pelicans, dolphins
DISTANCE: 106 miles (171 km)   **DIFFICULTY:** Easy

The multiuse Florida Keys Overseas Heritage Trail (FKOHT) runs parallel to U.S. Highway 1 for its entirety, tracing an old railroad line built by Henry Flagler, a notable developer of Florida's Atlantic coast, including Miami and Palm Beach. The FKOHT includes 42 bridges that connect all of the Florida Keys from Key Largo down to Key West.

The trail is a favorite among runners who live in the Keys. It's pancake flat (perfect for all kinds of workouts, whether an easy run or something faster that requires even terrain), with stunning views of the Atlantic Ocean as you traverse those bridges. The space can become so expansive that on a full-moon night, runners who have looked both ways might turn off their headlamp for a spell and let the glow of the moon completely light their way.

Along the trail, you'll see a lot of sites that most will miss while driving the interstate, including Everglades and Biscayne National Parks. The FKOHT also takes you through several marine and wildlife sanctuaries and 10 state parks.

If you make it the whole way down to Key West, you can touch the southernmost point of the continental United States, visit Ernest Hemingway's former home, and kick back to recover with a frozen drink in hand.

The trail contains access points to Everglades National Park, Biscayne National Park, Crocodile Lake National Wildlife Refuge, and a dozen other state parks.

CABO SAN LUCAS

Where the Pacific Ocean meets the Sea of Cortez

BEST TIME TO GO: December to February   **WHAT YOU'LL SEE:** Sea lions, birds
DISTANCE: Variable   **DIFFICULTY:** Easy to moderate

Cabo San Lucas is a resort town with a reputation for lively nightlife, but the area also offers its share of running options along the sea (and beyond). You just have to get enough sleep—and maybe go light on the frozen drinks—to enjoy them.

If you're looking for a flat, three- to four-mile (4.8-6.4 km) run, head to the marina early in the morning before it becomes crowded with tourists. Take in the private yachts, as well as the sea lions who tend to populate the area. Or for a bird's-eye view of Land's End, where the rock formation El Arco rises from the sea, head to the local Costco. Near the store, you'll find a dirt trail that climbs to a nearby summit with spectacular views that seem to go on forever. It's only a three-mile (4.8 km) out-and-back path, but it has a steep climb for spice.

If you're looking for more of a challenge, the Sierra de la Laguna mountain range is your best bet. It's just north of Cabo San Lucas and accessible by car. While it attracts runners, hikers, and mountain bikers, it feels remote compared to bustling Cabo San Lucas. The directions for the trail options can be a bit vague, so consider going through one of many tour companies and finding a guide to help plot out the adventure.

For a change of scenery, runners can explore San José del Cabo, about 20 miles (32 km) northeast of Cabo San Lucas. It's a more laid-back beach town, with the same sandy white shores and clear blue water, minus the hubbub of Los Cabos. You can run to the estuary, where you'll find a bird sanctuary harboring red-tailed hawks, herons, egrets, pelicans, and ospreys.

Take a detour from your running route to visit San José del Cabo Church.

INCA TRAIL

A multiday run to Machu Picchu's splendor

BEST TIME TO GO: May to October   **WHAT YOU'LL SEE:** Llamas, hummingbirds, condors, Inca Empire ruins
DISTANCE: 26 miles (42 km)   **DIFFICULTY:** Challenging

You could take a bus or train from Cusco to Machu Picchu, or you could run the Inca Trail (a route many take at more mild speeds). For experienced runners only, the 26-mile journey is achievable in three or four days at a safe pace. But the altitude of this trek fluctuates from a low of 6,561 feet (2,000 m) to a high of 13,828 feet (4,215 m), so give yourself time to acclimate and pay close attention to how you're feeling. The terrain is mountainous, spectacular, and technical. You might be tempted to fly through it (it's just a marathon, and you're there!), but with planning and foresight, you can glean more from one of the world's most historic trails.

The Inca Trail was used by the Inca emperor in the 15th century as a pilgrimage route to Machu Picchu, earning it the nickname Royal Road. While you're traversing this route, you'll experience several ecosystems, from alpine peaks to subtropical jungle. The area is strictly permitted, and you are required to go with a tour company or guide, so book an outfitter that allows running.

The first half of the run includes the most challenging leg of the journey: the climb over Dead Woman's Pass. Fortunately, it's not as ominous as it sounds—the silhouette of the mountain resembles a woman lying down. It will still test you, though. You'll ascend 3,937 feet (1,200 m) to the highest point on the Inca Trail, and at the top find a stunning view of the Andes.

The Inca Trail passes several significant Inca ruins, but it saves the most awe-inspiring for last: Machu Picchu. The ancient urban center lies amid the mountain's tropical forests, and the collision of ecosystems ensures an impression that will stay with you forever.

Whether you run or hike the Inca Trail, the route to Machu Picchu includes profound history and unbeatable views of the Andes.

SANDAKPHU-PHALUT TREK

A run on the border between Nepal and India

BEST TIME TO GO: Spring or fall   **WHAT YOU'LL SEE:** Bamboo and rhododendron forests
DISTANCE: 36 miles (58 km)   **DIFFICULTY:** Moderate

Getting to Sandakphu, the highest peak in the state of West Bengal, India, is a strenuous effort but a special treat. Nowhere else does a trail wind through flowering rhododendron forests, giant magnolias, and the largest concentration of orchids in the world. You might see red pandas, anteater-like pangolins, and epic views of Mount Everest too. For runners who don't mind slowing their pace or stopping for photos, the trek is a sweeping and stirring experience. Plan to travel in springtime for inspiring blooms and remarkable sunsets.

The Sandakphu-Phalut adventure can be broken up into segments, with overnight stays in lodges at several spots along the way. These lodges are often minimalist accommodations—don't expect running water or consistent electricity—though some places have more amenities than others. Nevertheless, even in the most minimal settings you will find welcoming hosts and hot, comforting food. A guide hired through a tour operator can be a useful resource for navigating the small villages along the trail.

The run begins in Manebhanjan, about 16 miles (26 km) from Darjeeling. The beginning of the trail is a climb gaining almost 3,000 feet (914 m) of elevation. It's a gradual ascent before the terrain levels out. Soon, you'll skirt the border between Nepal and India (carry your identification and documents with you to avoid hang-ups at the international checkpoints). Views

OPPOSITE: The Tonglu Trekkers' Hut in Darjeeling is a popular stopover for trail hikers or runners who take on the entire adventure.

PAGES 350-351: The verdant tea plantations in Munnar are an irresistible invitation to rest and take in the scenery.

of Kanchenjunga Peak, the third highest summit in the world, reward the navigation. The mountain, also known as the Sleeping Buddha for its distinguishable silhouette, is a reminder of peace and patience during a difficult leg of the trip.

The additional ascent to Sandakphu is not as difficult as the first climb, though altitude on the summit at 11,930 feet (3,636 m) can play a factor for less acclimated runners. At the top, you'll see four of the five highest peaks in the world: Everest, Kanchenjunga, Lhotse, and Makalu. From there, the exploration continues on to Phalut, the second highest peak of West Bengal, at around 11,800 feet (3,600 m). The final stretch to Sepi, through bamboo forests, might include a red panda sighting. Keep your eyes peeled as you near the end of your trail adventure, then prepare for a long nap—maybe on the six-hour drive back to the airport.

TRAVEL TIP

Sometimes the permitting requirements and lodging recommendations can be confusing, and a guide might be not only helpful but also required in certain areas. Look for registered guide associations and reputable tour companies, and get rates up front.

GEORGE S. MICKELSON TRAIL

A run through the legendary Black Hills

BEST TIME TO GO: May to September   **WHAT YOU'LL SEE:** Rock formations, 1890s-era train tunnels
DISTANCE: 108.8 miles (175.1 km)   **DIFFICULTY:** Easy

The Mickelson Trail begins in Edgemont, South Dakota, and travels over 100 miles north to Deadwood. Between, you'll see relics of the Wild West along the crushed limestone path. The route follows what was once the Black Hills Central Railroad—and is one of the country's most successful rails-to-trails initiatives. The trail is an accessible and enjoyable way for runners of all skill levels to enjoy Black Hills National Forest.

With 15 trailheads, it's easy to jump on and off the Mickelson Trail. The entire path features more than 100 railroad bridges and four rock tunnels. Although runners don't encounter any significant inclines, a gradual climb (about a 4 percent grade) from Dumont to Deadwood might challenge those looking for a more intense run.

Deadwood, a gold rush–era town founded in the 1870s, has retained its Wild West atmosphere while evolving into a hub for runners and other outdoor enthusiasts. Take a day in and around Deadwood, then build an itinerary to Mount Rushmore National Memorial or Custer State Park—both are in proximity to the Mickelson Trail.

Between the worst of the summer humidity and winter's first snowfall, early fall offers the best running weather in this part of the United States. Fall high temperatures in the Black Hills just touch 57°F (13.9°C). A run on the trail's Mystic-Rochford stretch offers the best foliage in autumn.

Sunset in the Black Hills creates an astonishing marriage of light and scenery, especially in fall.

PALO DURO CANYON

Where telltale red stains mark the canyon's trail runners

BEST TIME TO GO: Spring or fall   **WHAT YOU'LL SEE:** Lizards, coyotes, roadrunners
DISTANCE: Variable   **DIFFICULTY:** Challenging

Palo Duro Canyon is a trail runner's paradise tucked inside the Texas Panhandle, outside of Amarillo. Second in size only to the Grand Canyon among U.S. canyons, Palo Duro is drenched in color and majesty. The red rock and dirt serve as a backdrop to towering green junipers and earthy cacti. Prepare to take some of that color home with you too. The red dirt stains just about everything (wear dark sneakers or a pair you won't mind retiring at the end of the trip).

Palo Duro Canyon is about 120 miles (193 km) long, and 20 miles (32 km) at its widest point. There's a lot of ground to cover, but a popular trail run to get acquainted with the park is the Lighthouse Trail, which features the titular rock formation as the capstone of a 5.9-mile-long (9.5 km) out-and-back with a short climb. The views and colors are in full effect in late spring and early summer, but beware that in peak summer, canyon temperatures often top more than 100°F (37.8°C)—a sunrise run will help you beat the heat and grant you spectacular lighting.

If a race is the ideal way for you to explore the canyon, Palo Duro offers plenty of small trail races to tackle. The Palo Duro 25K Trail Run (15.5 miles), 50K (31 miles), and 50-miler (80.5 km) take place in October. With just over 200 finishers, the event has a strong community feel, and you have the added benefit of well-stocked aid stations along the course.

A 5.9-mile (9.5 km) out-and-back will bring you to the lighthouse, the signature formation of the park.

PERSEVERANCE TRAIL

A secluded adventure in gold rush wilderness

BEST TIME TO GO: June to August   **WHAT YOU'LL SEE:** Salmonberry bushes, waterfalls, possibly black bears
DISTANCE: 5 miles (8 km) round trip   **DIFFICULTY:** Moderate

The Perseverance Trail is thought to be one of the first roads ever built in Alaska. Originally, it served the area's booming mining industry (in the 1930s, the region produced an estimated $80 million in gold), and today, it stands as a fantastic running and hiking trail through the mountains surrounding Gold Creek Valley.

Although the area feels remote, it's quite accessible from downtown Juneau via Basin Road. The trail's first three-quarters of a mile (1.2 km) are uphill, and the route takes visitors along the mountainous ridges following Gold Creek. You may spot old mine shafts along the way (try to resist the urge to look for gold). Plenty of other trails connect to Perseverance at several junctures, so this is a good place for a flexible, spontaneous run where you can add mileage or a vertical challenge as you feel fit. Ebner Falls, where water thunders down about 200 feet (60 m) against rock steps, is worth a detour, as is Mount Juneau. The climb is steep, but not technical, and it takes just a little determination to reach the top. The trail is only about 1.5 miles (2.4 km) long, and you'll enjoy a vantage point from the 3,565-foot (1,087 m) summit. On a clear day, you might see cruise ships in Juneau's port, the Chilkat River, and Lemon Creek Glacier.

Juneau is only accessible by plane or boat, making it a place worth investing in once you arrive. The best (and most popular) time to go is during summer, when wildflowers decorate the lush forest, temperatures top out in the mid-60s Fahrenheit (around 18°C), and runners can enjoy 18 hours of daylight.

TRAVEL TIP

Don't forget to pack your rain gear. Although summer is Alaska's driest season, Juneau still lies in the "rain belt" and is considered a temperate rainforest.

Perseverance's main trail offers views of the ridgelines. Occasionally, rockslides can make the path more technical than expected, so wear sturdy shoes.

PRE'S TRAIL

An icon's footsteps in Tracktown, U.S.A.

BEST TIME TO GO: July to October   **WHAT YOU'LL SEE:** University of Oregon students, many runners
DISTANCE: 4 miles (6.4 km)   **DIFFICULTY:** Easy

You're likely already well acquainted with the epicenter of U.S. track and field—Eugene, Oregon. You'll find running iconography and history at every turn in this home to several shoe companies, elite run clubs, and the University of Oregon's legendary Hayward Field. Pre's Trail is the cultural center of running in Eugene. Noted for its wood chip surface, which will leave your shoes an earthy reddish color, the trail is named in honor of Steve "Pre" Prefontaine, a legendary running talent known for his epic accomplishments in the 1,500 meters and 10,000 meters. Pre died in a tragic car crash in 1975; the trail was completed that same year and designated a city historic landmark in 2019.

Today, runners of all skill levels use the route heavily, and the trail connects to others along the Willamette River and around the University of Oregon campus. On Pre's Trail, you can find a one- to four-mile (1.6–6.4 km) loop that passes through wetlands, green meadows, and woodlands. The trail is off of Martin Luther King Jr. Boulevard, near the university's Autzen Stadium, and traverses Alton Baker Park.

Eugene is the ideal place to find running inspiration or tap into your running "why" during a dogged season of training or after a setback. You might spot professional or NCAA athletes warming up on the trail alongside weekend warriors, beginners, and runners of all ages. You can also visit the town to watch a meet. Hayward Field hosts the prestigious Pre Classic each year, in addition to the NCAA championships and the Olympic trials.

WHILE YOU'RE THERE

Many visitors make a pilgrimage to Pre's Rock while in Eugene. The area on Skyline Boulevard marks the spot of Prefontaine's fatal accident. Fans continue to honor his legacy, leaving remembrances, flowers, cards, and even running shoes there.

Eugene has no shortage of running options, but Pre's Trail offers running history in a remote setting.

RED ROCK CANYON

Look out for dinosaurs just a half hour from the legendary Strip.

BEST TIME TO GO: Winter, spring, or late fall   **WHAT YOU'LL SEE:** Petroglyphs, seasonal waterfalls
DISTANCE: Variable   **DIFFICULTY:** Moderate

Standing in the middle of the Las Vegas Strip, you'd be hard-pressed to imagine that a wilderness oasis for trail runners exists a mere 30 minutes from all the neon and slot machines. But Red Rock Canyon beckons from the nearby Mojave Desert. Rent a car and take a break from the noise to get in a run. (Rideshare services can get you to Red Rock Canyon, but cell service might be spotty for organizing a return trip.)

Red Rock Canyon is best enjoyed outside the summer season, when it feels more like an oven than paradise. The canyon has multiple trails to choose from depending on your goals. The Grand Circle Loop is about 11 miles (17.7 km) across the desert foothills and over washes, and it starts right from the visitors center. If you're looking for a short but challenging adventure, the Ice Box Canyon Trail takes you 2.2 miles (3.5 km) through a cool, shady box canyon featuring otherworldly waterfalls, depending on seasonal rainfall. This one requires a bit of scrambling on boulders and loose rocks. The White Rock Mountain Loop is another option that splits the difference. It totals about six miles (9.7 km), but it takes you farther off the beaten path, offers more seclusion, and starts with a descent of 1,000 feet (305 m).

Throughout Red Rock Canyon, keep an eye out for dinosaur tracks in the Aztec sandstone. Traces from small, two-footed dinos have been located in the park, but the exact locations are not publicized because these are now protected fossils. For a certain landmark, check out the Keystone Thrust, a fault that formed about 65 million years ago, around the same time that dinosaurs went extinct. Truly no historic run rivals Red Rock in sheer scale.

Whether you run the six-mile (9.7 km) White Rock Loop or 11-mile (17.7 km) Grand Circle Loop, you won't believe you're just minutes from the Vegas Strip.

FORÊT DE LA PROVIDENCE

A hidden trail-running hot spot in the Indian Ocean

BEST TIME TO GO: May to October   **WHAT YOU'LL SEE:** A volcano   **DISTANCE:** Variable
DIFFICULTY: Moderate to challenging

Réunion Island is best described as a mountain sitting in the ocean. This under-the-radar region, just 39 miles (63 km) long and 28 miles (45 km) wide, has a thriving running scene, offering more than 600 miles (965 km) of trails to explore.

But first, you have to know how to reach the island. It's actually nowhere near France. In fact, Réunion Island is an overseas department in the western Indian Ocean, about 420 miles (680 km) east of Madagascar and 110 miles (180 km) southwest of Mauritius. A nonstop flight from the East Coast of the United States will take 22 to 30 hours to the airport in Saint-Denis, the capital city of Réunion Island. A flight from France, meanwhile, is 11 hours. When you finally reach this little-known gem, an unmatched adventure awaits you on its white and black sandy beaches, and lush, mountainous interior.

With so many trails, your run could start almost as soon as you get off the plane. Take a four-mile (6.4 km) jaunt along the Forêt de la Providence as a sneak peek of what to expect during the rest of your trail-running vacation. The terrain is technical all over—expect a lot of rocks and roots underfoot—but the options are endless. Add the active volcano Piton de la Fournaise to your must-see list with a nine-mile (14.5 km) run on volcanic rock and ash formed by lava flows. You can access it from the Pas de Bellecombe trailhead, at about 7,710 feet (2,350 m) above sea level.

The mineral surfaces around Piton de la Fournaise are unlike anywhere else on Earth. Just watch your step—the ground can be slippery after a foggy morning.

RIM TO RIM TO RIM

Preparation is the key to success on this Grand Canyon double crossing challenge.

BEST TIME TO GO: October   **WHAT YOU'LL SEE:** Two billion years of geological history
DISTANCE: 41 to 48 miles (66-77 km)   **DIFFICULTY:** Challenging

Although five million people visit the Grand Canyon every year, less than one percent hike below the rim of this natural wonder of the world. Views from the top of the canyon do much to communicate its unfathomable vastness, but true magic and sacredness await runners who dip below.

For trail runners, the Grand Canyon is nothing but exploration and potential. The ultimate challenge is traversing the rugged terrain between the South and North Rims twice over in what's known as the Rim to Rim to Rim journey. The intense climbs and descents will test you in ways nowhere else in the world can.

You have a few route options for completing the Rim to Rim to Rim, but numbers can only approximate the experience. First, you'll descend 4,860 feet (1,480 m) over 6.3 miles (10.1 km), then ascend 6,000 feet (1,829 m) over 14.3 miles (23 km), then repeat in the other direction. The boldest of trail runners try the Rim to Rim to Rim in one day, over the course of 10 hours or more (ignoring the copious signs from the National Park Service that advise against this). Whether you're attempting the challenge in one day or several, you'll feel the accomplishment deep in your legs and your soul.

The layers of ancient rock, surge of the Colorado River, looming natural formations—all are enough to intimidate, humble, and inspire you to new heights of running achievement. Take breathers as needed so you can appreciate the landscape and its significance to what we know about ourselves and our planet; you wouldn't want to rush on these narrow trails anyway.

TRAVEL TIP

Most runners start and finish on the South Rim, which offers more amenities like grocery stores and accommodations (Tusayan, at the entrance to the park, has hotels, and the park has lodges). The North Rim is more remote, and its lodges and campground close between October and May.

OPPOSITE: Late fall, before it snows, is ideal for any Rim to Rim to Rim attempt.

PAGES 366-367: Ascending via the South Kaibab Trail is a brutal final challenge for those who started on the other end at the Bright Angel Trail.

Preparation is critical to a successful double crossing of the Grand Canyon. To undertake this arduous run, train like you would for a race. Incorporate stairs, steps, hills, slopes—whatever prepares your hamstrings for the ascents and your quads for the descents. Run at all times, in all weather too. The climate inside the canyon can be very different from the climate on the ridge. Snow and ice can appear in winter months, heat can compound into a debilitating run stopper, and monsoons can hit fast and without warning. It's critical to stay attuned to the environment—consider a trail run without headphones—and heed Park Service advisories.

The shortest Rim to Rim to Rim route is about 41 miles (66 km), taking the South Kaibab Trail to the North Kaibab Trail, and back. An alternative, which adds about seven miles (11 km) but lets you see more of the canyon, utilizes the Bright Angel Trail on the South Rim, which also has stations to refill a water bottle or hydration pack. Both routes bottom out at the only lodging beneath the rim, Phantom Ranch, on the north side of the

GEAR CHECK

The trails in the canyon are mostly smooth, but you'll still want trail shoes with cushion and traction. Make sure you have a hydration vest that provides at least a day's worth of fluids and has pockets for essentials like snacks, a first aid kit, your ID, cash, a waterproof shell, gloves, headwear, eyewear, a headlamp, and extra socks.

ABOVE: For those who don't want to speed through the canyon floor, try to snag a spot at Phantom Ranch, a once-in-a-lifetime stay.

OPPOSITE: Toroweap Point is the only place in the national park where you can enjoy a vertical view of the Colorado River.

Colorado River. It's a great place to rest, soak your legs in the river, and refuel before heading up in either direction (a small canteen by the river is open to the public most of the year). If you want to split your run into two days, you can also try to reserve a bed at Phantom Ranch—they serve a family-style barbecue meal in the evening—but space is extremely limited and only afforded by lottery, so plan ahead of time.

As the Rim to Rim to Rim has become an increasingly popular runner challenge, park rangers have started looking out for those daring enough to try the run. Running the route is not strictly prohibited, but the park does have your safety in mind, and rangers might stop you to advise on the day's conditions, weather, or anything else that might affect your safety. Listen to their warnings and wait for a better day—every step in the Grand Canyon is worth it.

PARQUE FORESTAL AND BEYOND

Run easy in the city, run long in the mountains.

BEST TIME TO GO: September to February   **WHAT YOU'LL SEE:** Andes Mountains, intriguing architecture
DISTANCE: Variable   **DIFFICULTY:** Easy

Santiago, Chile, resides in one of the most unique geographical locales in the world, right beneath the snowcapped Andes Mountains and just about 50 miles (80 km) from the sparkling beaches along the Pacific Ocean. For runners, the diversity presents a massive array of backdrops, styles, and destinations to sample during a trip to one of the most active cities in the Southern Hemisphere.

The streets of Santiago aren't the most accommodating to runners, but the city offers pockets of green space for those who want to string together shorter routes (up to seven miles [11.3 km] long) in the midst of sightseeing and more relaxed modes of travel. Santiago's Parque O'Higgins has the feel of New York's Central Park (page 316), with an outer loop that will net you about 2.3 miles (3.7 km) per go-around and help you find your bearings in the urban center. Parque Forestal, on the other hand, runs along the Mapocho River, between Plaza Baquedano and Estación Mapocho. This park has dirt paths and routes that stretch up to seven miles (11.3 km).

Outside of Santiago, running options abound in the mountains if you have a car or are willing to take public transportation. If you drive three hours southeast of the city, you'll reach El Morado Natural Monument in Cajón del Maipo, where you can take a 10-mile (16.1 km) hike to see San Francisco Glacier, El Volcán River Basin, a lagoon, and hot springs.

Araucano Park offers expansive skyline views of Santiago.

STANLEY PARK SEAWALL

Miles of waterfront in a convenient loop

BEST TIME TO GO: Spring or fall **WHAT YOU'LL SEE:** English Bay, rabbits, beavers, coyotes
DISTANCE: 6.2 miles (10 km) **DIFFICULTY:** Easy

Vancouver, nestled between the Pacific Ocean and the North Shore Mountains, is a city teeming with fitness and outdoor recreation enthusiasts. You'll find plenty of places to run, but don't miss the Stanley Park Seawall and its view of English Bay.

Once you've entered Stanley Park, you can almost forget you're in a city at all. A miniature forest, gorgeous gardens, and a natural west coast rainforest await. The concrete path around the park is 6.2 miles (10 km) of nearly uninterrupted waterfront. You'll travel through lighthouse tower archways, take in views of Burrard Inlet and the Vancouver Aquarium, catch glimpses of the North Shore Mountains, and see the Lions Gate Bridge, one of the world's longest suspension bridges. The route features separate paths for walkers, runners, and cyclists at many points, so you won't have to worry much about navigating unpredictable crowds. Travel on the path is one-way too.

After your run, relax on one of two beaches in the park. Runners will also want to stop at the Harry Jerome statue, just past Hallelujah Point, which pays homage to one of Canada's all-time great sprinters, a bronze medalist at the 1964 Olympics who set seven world records during his career.

Stanley Park is also home to more than 200 bird species, great for those hobbyists pulling double duty on the run. Just be sure to give the Canada geese a wide berth.

Large maple trees show off their fall colors in Stanley Park.

SYDNEY OLYMPIC PARK

An Olympic track and professional-grade trails

BEST TIME TO GO: September to November or March to May   **WHAT YOU'LL SEE:** Sports recreation venues, meadows, green parkways   **DISTANCE:** Variable   **DIFFICULTY:** Easy

After cities host the Olympics, the facilities built for the games often become abandoned eyesores. But decades after the 2000 Summer Games, Olympic Park in Sydney, Australia, continues to thrive. Today, it's an epicenter for sports, recreation, and cultural events, attracting more than 12 million visitors each year.

Runners will find 22 miles (35 km) of multiuse pathways throughout the park, providing space for peaceful shakeout and training runs uninterrupted by traffic. Located about eight miles (13 km) west of central Sydney, the area is accessible by train or car. Although you can configure any route that suits your desires, the main circuits offer distances of 3.4 miles (5.5 km), 4.8 miles (7.7 km), and 6.9 miles (11.1 km). The park also features a fully equipped track facility, perfect for intervals and speed work.

Olympic Park also has several lookout points for when you want to catch your breath. Of note: The Woo-la-ra (Aboriginal for "lookout place") is near the riverside area and features twisting paths to a summit, where you'll find a nice vantage point to see the Sydney skyline at the Newington Nature Reserve.

Sydney offers a lot to see on the run besides Olympic Park. Follow the local marathon course for views of Bondi Beach and Sydney Harbour as well as the famous Sydney Opera House and the Royal Botanic Garden. Bondi Beach boasts a breezy four-mile (6.4 km) path to thoroughly relish the coastline.

Run along the famous Bondi Beach and listen to the sounds of waves lapping the shore.

TABLE MOUNTAIN NATIONAL PARK

One of South Africa's most photographed landmarks

BEST TIME TO GO: January to March **WHAT YOU'LL SEE:** Table Mountain ghost frogs, Atlantic Ocean
DISTANCE: Variable **DIFFICULTY:** Challenging

t's easy to see where Table Mountain got its name. The mountain's steep cliffs loom over Cape Town and the Atlantic Ocean, then completely flatten out on top to form a two-mile-long (3.2 km) plateau. A cable car has made the summit an easy-to-reach hot spot for tourists, but runners will find plenty of hiking and running trails for a one-of-a-kind challenge—particularly given Table Mountain's altitude at 3,563 feet (1,086 m).

The Platteklip Gorge Trail is the most direct route to the top of Table Mountain. It starts on Tafelberg Road and skirts west of Maclear's Beacon, the mountain's highest point, while gaining 2,000 feet (610 m) in just 1.5 miles (2.4 km) via rocky steps and trail. The grade is steep, but several lookout points make the top more than just a quick photograph. If you want a longer route, another popular option is the climb up nearby Devil's Peak, also starting from Tafelberg Road. The Devil's Peak path stretches 4.3 miles (7 km) on a zigzagging trail, then deposits you at a summit featuring a 360-degree view of Cape Town, as well as Table Mountain. You may run into Indian gray mongooses or rock hyraxes, among other wildlife, along the way.

With so many routes to choose from, you may wear yourself out on Table Mountain. The good news is that the cable car option is still on the table (so to speak). Hitch a ride back down the mountain and find yourself some bunny chow (hollowed-out bread stuffed with curry, kidney beans, or meat).

Along the trail up Table Mountain, keep your eyes peeled—the landmark features more than 6,000 species of bush plants.

TAHOE RIM TRAIL

A maximalist runner's dream

BEST TIME TO GO: July to September **WHAT YOU'LL SEE:** Alpine lakes, waterfalls, mountain peaks, conifer forests, wildflowers **DISTANCE:** 165 miles (266 km) **DIFFICULTY:** Moderate to challenging

When many runners start planning to explore the Tahoe Rim Trail, they must first answer: Where to begin? The 165-mile route circumnavigates Lake Tahoe. It passes through California and Nevada, overlaps with the Pacific Crest Trail, and dips into no less than three national forests. It's a lot of ground to cover for even the boldest trail runners, whether you're planning to do the entire trail, break it into segments, or go out for a day trip.

Lake Tahoe itself—about 22 miles (35 km) long and 12 miles (19 km) wide—is a site to see. The fresh water is perfectly blue, surrounded by the gorgeous snowcapped Sierra Nevada mountains. The Rim Trail allows for several different perspectives of this beautiful body of water, as well as other alpine lakes along the way. The entire route is at high altitude—the lowest point is 6,200 feet (1,890 m) in Tahoe City while the highest is 10,300 feet (3,140 m) at the top of Nevada's Relay Peak in the northeast section.

Many thru-hikers and runners start the trek in Tahoe City and travel clockwise to save the stunning Desolation Wilderness for last. If you're only going to see one segment of the entire trail, Desolation ranks high as your best option, boasting a rugged granite landscape, subalpine forests, and glacially formed lakes.

For those who dare to take on the entire 165 miles, camping is available all along the trail. But plan your water sources carefully ahead of time. The east shore is notably dry, with few options for restocking without going a mile or

OPPOSITE: If the trail run doesn't wear you out, Emerald Bay State Park offers kayaking to the island in Emerald Bay.

PAGES 380-381: Everyone— from day hikers to backpackers to ultrarunners— takes on the rim trail.

more out of your way. Some trail conquerors plan the excursion with a (super) supportive friend. These runners create preplanned segments, where their support team will pick them up as they finish at the checkpoint for that day's run, then drop them off the next day to resume the mission. It's a great way to see the whole trail without having to do a lot of resource management, so long as you don't mind more logistical planning. Bold trail runners used to long runs aim to finish in about eight days—with runs ranging from 16 to 33 miles (26–53 km) in a day, including the Desolation Wilderness stretch.

What makes the Tahoe Rim Trail special is the diversity of its landscape and numerous access points that can accommodate anyone—from experienced trail trekkers and their support crews to beginners just dipping their feet into the trail scene. The entire area is a dream for all runners, whether seeking a quick out-and-back jog or a 165-mile odyssey.

RUNNING TIP

Trail angels sometimes come to the rescue along thru-hike areas like the Tahoe Rim Trail. These kindly people leave water and other necessities for future runners who may be in need. If you're in a pinch and are out of fuel or water, a trail angel package could bail you out. On the other hand, if you finish your run with more than you need, consider leaving your extra supplies behind and becoming a trail angel yourself.

WICHITA MOUNTAINS WILDLIFE REFUGE

Where bison and longhorns make for surprisingly enjoyable running buddies

---

BEST TIME TO GO: Summer or fall **WHAT YOU'LL SEE:** Lizards, hedgehogs, prairie dogs, deer, bison, cattle
DISTANCE: Variable **DIFFICULTY:** Moderate

Nestled in the Wichita Mountains of southwestern Oklahoma is a wildlife refuge where trail runners can find a unique setting to log miles. The Wichita Mountains Wildlife Refuge has become a favorite for locals who enjoy looking for bison or long-horned cattle while traversing pathways through wildflower-strewn prairies, lakes, and woodlands.

You won't be short of places to explore: The area has 20 different trails through its 59,020 acres (23,885 ha). You can string together shorter trails to come up with more mileage, or head to French Lake on the intermediate six-mile (9.7 km) Bison Trail.

The route has nice vistas of the mountains in the background, but keep your eyes on the open prairie and you'll likely see much of the namesake wildlife. Bison roam on the open range, along with some elk and longhorns. These sightings are the charm of running in the refuge, and the flat, non-technical terrain means you can soak in the sights instead of fussing over the trail (though the mountain granite can occasionally make pathways rocky).

If you want to tackle a three-mile uphill run (about 10 km round trip) in Wichita, go to Mount Scott on the eastern side of the refuge. It's approximately a 7 percent incline on a paved road. At the overlook, take in the view of Lake Lawtonka. Nearby is the town of Medicine Park, a quaint, visitor-friendly place to relax and eat after a long day outside.

The peak of Elk Mountain makes for stunning photo opportunities.

FOREST PARK

Miles of trails in an outdoorsy wonderland

BEST TIME TO GO: Year-round   **WHAT YOU'LL SEE: Douglas firs, orange honeysuckles, salmonberries, grouse, great horned owls, flying squirrels**   **DISTANCE: Variable**   **DIFFICULTY: Easy to moderate**

The tree-dense northwest section of Portland, Oregon, conceals a massive network of trails perfect for outdoor enthusiasts. Forest Park spans some 5,200 acres (2,100 ha) flanked by the Willamette River to its east. It proudly serves as an air and water filter for the region—and with more than 80 miles (129 km) of trails, Portland's runners flock there.

The anchor of Forest Park's trail system is the Wildwood Trail, which is 30 miles (48.3 km) long, parallel to Leif Erikson Drive. The nontechnical, dirt single-track route is lined by thick ferns in the spring. The southern end begins at the Vietnam Veterans Memorial in Washington Park, then the trail heads northwest before ending at Newberry Road. The undulating terrain overlooks the Willamette River for stretches, twisting through a deep forest of big-leaf maples. At the trail's highest point sits the Pittock Mansion (the 1914 home of publisher Henry Pittock and his wife, Georgiana), where clear days treat you to views of the Cascade Mountains, including Mount Hood, as well as the Columbia-Willamette confluence.

Leif Erikson Drive is an 11-mile (17.7 km) gravel route from NW Thurman Street to NW Germantown Road. If you're feeling strong, you can start here and spin off onto many of the connected trails that extend throughout the park. Looping together the Maple and Wildwood Trails makes for a pleasant seven-mile (11.3 km) outing, highlighted by Douglas fir trees, creeks, and a few canyons too. And if you want something short and easy, opt for the

OPPOSITE: The Witch's Castle (gulp!) connects the Wildwood Trail to the Lower Macleay trailhead.

PAGES 386-387: The denseness of the forest can be surprising near downtown Portland, but the trail is accommodating and double wide.

Skyline Cruise Loop. At less than three miles (4.8 km), it's short enough to fit into a busy travel schedule but long enough to break a sweat and catch views of those serene snowcapped mountains in the distance.

Forest Park is welcoming to runners who visit Portland for business or racing or otherwise. You won't encounter any technical terrain, and maintenance in the park is so consistent that you don't need trail running shoes—regular running shoes will do. Even on a typically rainy Portland day, the dense tree canopy overhead serves as shelter against the precipitation. One word of caution: For Forest Park newbies, the area can become a little disorienting due to the zigzagging pattern of the trails. Take your phone or a paper map just in case you get turned around. The park is a nice place to spend time, but Portland has so much to offer, you surely don't want to spend *all* of your time there.

TRAVEL TIP

Coffee and running go hand in hand, and Portland is an Eden for both. Ditch the chains and instead sample the independent shops roasting their own beans. Cathedral Coffee on Willamette Boulevard is right across the river from Forest Park, or try Nossa Familia Coffee in the Pearl District for flavors from founder Augusto Carneiro's native Brazil.

WISSAHICKON VALLEY PARK

A creekside wilderness near Center City

BEST TIME TO GO: Spring, summer, or fall   **WHAT YOU'LL SEE:** Owls, chickadees, woodpeckers
DISTANCE: Variable   **DIFFICULTY:** Easy

Wissahickon Valley Park in Northwest Philadelphia is a gem for urban dwellers, offering 50 miles (80.5 km) of rugged trails. For runners, it's a change of pace from a busy East Coast corridor and more than worth a day trip from Philadelphia.

The pathways in Wissahickon Valley Park are protected under dense forests, and wind through open meadows and alongside creeks. For a wide, flat gravel trail, runners choose the five-mile (8 km) Forbidden Drive next to Wissahickon Creek. It's called Forbidden Drive because motorized vehicles aren't allowed, so run worry free.

If you want to reach Forbidden Drive from Center City Philadelphia and extend your run altogether, hop on the Schuylkill River Trail and Lincoln Drive Trail, which connect the park to downtown. Another opportunity to add mileage from Forbidden Drive itself is via Wissahickon's single-track trails. These can be a bit rugged and hilly, so they're an effective way to add challenge to your outing.

If you're looking for a bite after your run, go to the Valley Green Inn and soak up a little bit of local history with your recovery meal. The last of the roadhouses and taverns that once populated this area in the 1800s, it's now a favorite brunch spot; try to score a seat on the front porch, where you can watch runners, hikers, and cyclists whiz by.

The crushed stone on Forbidden Drive is friendliest with trail shoes.

WONDERLAND TRAIL

The crown jewel of Cascadia

BEST TIME TO GO: Summer **WHAT YOU'LL SEE:** Wildflowers, marmots, glaciers
DISTANCE: 93 miles (150 km) **DIFFICULTY:** Challenging

At the center of the epic journey around the Wonderland Trail is snowcapped Mount Rainier. Climbing Rainier's 14,410 feet (4,392 m) is its own adventure, but Wonderland is ideal for runners in search of something grand. The route through Mount Rainier National Park stretches 93 magnificent miles (150 km) and encompasses 22,810 feet (6,953 m) of vertical gain and loss as it travels through forestland, vibrant wildflower-strewn meadows, and ridges left by area glaciers.

Though some runners choose to tackle the entire route over several days or weeks, others opt to explore the park in sections. The Mystic Lake to Sunrise Camp segment on the northeast side is among the most popular for those looking to make a day trip. It's a 10.6-mile (17.1 km) jaunt that includes navigating lateral moraines, the rocks and debris left behind by melting glaciers. This segment includes views of Winthrop Glacier, the second largest in the area, and takes you across Winthrop Creek. At Skyscraper Pass, you can add on a short climb to the top of Skyscraper Mountain if you want to see what 7,000 feet (2,134 m) of altitude feels like. As with all the sections of the Wonderland Trail, expect some steep climbs and comparable descents.

The most popular time to visit the Wonderland Trail is mid-July through mid-September. The driest months are July and August, but the Pacific Northwest can host rain at any time, so be prepared. No matter the weather, the scenery is among the most awe-inspiring and the trail is well maintained, calling out to runners to explore this breathtaking landscape.

You'll never be out of sight of Mount Rainier on the Wonderland Trail.

RUNS BY DESTINATION

ACKNOWLEDGMENTS

Writing a book is like an ultramarathon. It takes a great team to get you to the finish line. Thanks for the editing and guidance from my former *Runner's World* colleagues David Willey and Erin Strout. So nice to work with you again. And it is quite the honor to work with the professional team at National Geographic, including executive editor Allyson Johnson, associate editor Tyler Daswick, designer Jerry Sealy, and photo editor Katie Dance. Thanks for making my running dream come to fruition.

ABOUT THE AUTHOR

Bart Yasso is the former chief running officer of *Runner's World* magazine. He is unofficially known as the "Mayor of Running," having drawn countless athletes into the sport through his ambassadorship and appearances at races around the world. He is one of the few people to have completed races on all seven continents, including the Antarctica Marathon and the Kilimanjaro Marathon. He has also completed the Badwater ultramarathon, a 135-mile (217.3 km) run through Death Valley, California, and is a five-time Ironman. He is an inductee into the Running USA Hall of Champions and the Road Runners Club of America Distance Running Hall of Fame. He is based in the Lehigh Valley, Pennsylvania.

ILLUSTRATIONS CREDITS

Cover, Dan Patitucci; back cover, Schneider Electric Marathon de Paris/A.S.O./Jonathan Biche; 2–3, Dan Patitucci; 4–5, Kevin Morris; 6–7, Maratona do Rio; 9, Big Sur Marathon courtesy of Bart Yasso; 10–1, Marathon des Sables; 12–3, Zac Zinn; 14–5, Jesse Peters/Backlight Photography; 17, SWKrull-Imaging/iStock Editorial/Getty Images; 18–9, Parker Seibold/The Gazette; 20–1, Sean Pavone Photo/Adobe Stock; 23, André Morgan; 24–5, Harold Stiver/Adobe Stock; 27, Mlenny/iStock/Getty Images; 28–9, Douglas Zimmerman; 31, Nick Fox/Adobe Stock; 32–3, The Bloomsday Run; 35–7, Gameface Media; 39, Haizhan Zheng/iStock/Getty Images; 40–1, © David H. Enzel, 2022; 43, Grace Beahm Alford/The Post and Courier; 44–5, jdross75/Adobe Stock; 47, Sean Pavone Photo/Adobe Stock; 48–9, Times-Picayune/Scott Threlkeld; 51, Orjan F. Ellingvag/Corbis via Getty Images; 53, MarkD2323/Adobe Stock; 54, courtesy The Captain Kidd; 55, Falmouth Road Race, Inc.; 57, Noah Densmore/Shutterstock; 58–9, Luis Santana; 60–1, Douglas R. Clifford/Tampa Bay Times via ZUMA Wire/Alamy Stock Photo; 63, AP Photo/Journal Inquirer, Irena Pastorello; 64–5, Jim Michaud/Journal Inquirer via AP; 67–9, Jesse Peters/Backlight Photography; 71–2, Joe Viger; 73, Diana Robinson Photography/Moment/Getty Images; 75, Darryl Brooks/Alamy Stock Photo; 76–7, Gene Phillips Photography; 78, Paul McPherson; 79, Blulz60/Alamy Stock Photo; 80–1, Schneider Electric Marathon de Paris/A.S.O./Jonathan Biche; 83, Luis Escobar/Big Sur Marathon; 84–5, Matthew Borowick; 86, Reg Regalado/MossMedia; 87, Luis Escobar/Big Sur Marathon; 89, Jino Lee/Stocksy; 90–1, Bruno Coelho/ Alamy Stock Photo; 92, Paopano/Shutterstock; 93, SOPA Images/Alamy Stock Photo; 95, Radlab for The IRONMAN Group; 97–9, Zurich Marató Barcelona; 101, Luciano Lima/Getty Images Sport; 102–4, SCC EVENTS/Tilo Wiedensohler [camera4]; 105, SCC EVENTS/Sebastian Wells [OSTKREUZ]; 107, Ashley Kaye/Adobe Stock; 108–9, Tony Bean of TABfotos; 110, Barry Davis/robertharding; 111, Tony Bean of TABfotos; 113–7, Kevin Morris; 119–21, Dave Holland Photography; 123, Taneos Ramsay/Cayman Compass; 125–7, Bank of America Chicago Marathon; 129, Michael Reaves/Getty Images Sport; 131, Copyright 2019 The Walt Disney Company; 132–3, The Walt Disney Company; 135, Madrugada Verde/Adobe Stock; 136–7, Ramsey Cardy/Sportsfile; 138, Sam Barnes/Sportsfile; 139, courtesy of The Irish Times; 141–3, Albatros Adventure Marathons; 145, Hanoi Marathon; 147, BMW Helsinki Marathon/Peetu Sillanpää, IG: pe.etu; 148, BMW Helsinki Marathon/Niklas Holmberg; 149, Dmitry Naumov/Adobe Stock; 151, Kyo46/Adobe Stock; 152–3, Honolulu Marathon Association; 155, Evren Kalinbacak/Shutterstock; 157, Dave McKay; 158–9, Westend61/Fotofeeling/Getty Images; 160–1, Jo Evans—Da Kine Images; 163, TTstudio/Adobe Stock; 164–5, James Schwabel/Alamy Stock Photo; 166–7, Maratona Clube de Portugal; 169, Twende Photography/Adobe Stock; 170, Lewa Safari Marathon; 171, spiritofamerica/Adobe Stock; 173, Ashok Saxena/Alamy Stock Photo; 174–5, Alex Davidson/Getty Images; 176, f11photo/Adobe Stock; 177, Alex Davidson/Getty Images Sport; 179, David Brownell/Alamy Stock Photo; 180, David Lyons/Alamy Stock Photo; 181, Sandy

Macys; 183, AMCM/Mainguy; 184–5, Nicolas Tucat/AFP via Getty Images; 186–7, AMCM/Mainguy; 189, @MissoulaMarathon; 191, Simon & Michael Ganz/Alamy Stock Photo; 192–3, Action Photo SA on behalf of The Kilimanjaro Marathon; 195, rudi1976/Adobe Stock; 197, Eduardo Munoz/Reuters/Redux; 198–9, AP Photo/Brittainy Newman; 200, Gordon Donovan/NurPhoto via AP; 201, AP Photo/Andres Kudacki; 203, Schneider Electric Marathon de Paris/A.S.O./Jonathan Biche; 204–5, SCStock/Adobe Stock; 206, Schneider Electric Marathon de Paris/A.S.O./Jonathan Biche; 207, Schneider Electric Marathon de Paris/A.S.O./Maxime Delobel; 209–11, JPG Photo & Video; 213, boyloso/Adobe Stock; 214–5, Bjarki Johanns; 217, Maratona do Rio; 219–21, Cecilia Fabiano/LaPresse via AP; 222, Alex Kane/Dreamstime; 223, sportpoint/Alamy Stock Photo; 225, Vanessa Newton/J&A Racing; 227–9, Zackery Wilson; 231, adidas Stockholm Marathon/Jonas Persson; 232–3, adidas Stockholm Marathon/Karolin Engman; 235, Ben Levy/Sydney Marathon; 237–40, Tokyo Marathon Foundation; 241, Taras Vyshnya—stock.adobe; 243, Canada Running Series; 245–9, Matt Cecill; 250–1, tonywithasony; 253, Rajesh Jantilal/AFP via Getty Images; 254–7, Comrades Marathon (CMA); 259–61, Kevin McGarry, courtesy Marathon Tours & Travel; 263, Nick Fox/Alamy Stock Photo; 265, Scott Stolarz/SCS Photoworks; 266–7, Niebrugge Images/Alamy Stock Photo; 268, Scott Stolarz/SCS Photoworks; 269, Matthew Micah Wright/The Image Bank/Getty Images; 271, Marathon des Sables; 273, tonywithasony; 275, Nathan Herde/Hood to Coast Relay; 276–7, LOOK-foto/Image Professionals GmbH/Alamy Stock Photo; 279, Ali Engin; 281, Pete Peterson; 282–3, Joe Azze; 285, Jungfrau-Marathon/David Birri; 287, David Freeman; 289, Jeff Pachoud/AFP via Getty Images; 290–1, AP Photo/Laurent Cipriani; 293, Parker Seibold/The Gazette; 294–5, Jon Watt © JWatt Photography; 296–7, Parker Seibold/The Gazette; 299, Luke Walker; 301, Jesse Ellis of Let's Wander Photography; 302–5, Hilary Yang; 306–7, Meghan Maloney; 309, Russ Bishop/Alamy Stock Photo; 310–1, Prisma by Dukas/UIG/Getty Images; 312, Per Breiehagen/Stone/Getty Images; 313, Jeff Pelletier (Instagram: @jpelletier); 315, Ian Dagnall/Alamy Stock Photo; 317, Jonathan Heisler; 318–9, Ben Rayner/The New York Times/Redux; 321, Moritz Wolf/imageBROKER/Alamy Stock Photo; 323, Frankie Spontelli; 325, Ben Herndon/TandemStock; 326–7, Lars Schneider/TandemStock; 329, George H. H. Huey; 331, olyphotostories/Adobe Stock; 332–3, Odyssey Stock/Stocksy; 335, Penny Chen/500px/Getty Images; 336–7, Ron Niebrugge/Alamy Stock Photo; 339, Kitti Boonnitrod/Moment/Getty Images; 341, Luke Tuttle, author of *Ultrarunning Europe*; 343, ByDroneVideos/Adobe Stock; 345, angeldibilio/Adobe Stock; 347, Danilo Rubini; 349, happystock/Adobe Stock; 350–1, Svitlana Belinska/Adobe Stock; 353, Stephen Taylor/Alamy Stock Photo; 355, Kip/Adobe Stock; 357, LouieLea/Shutterstock; 359, Dennis Dimick; 361, Kevin Youngblood; 363, Henner Damke/Adobe Stock; 365, Andy Cochrane; 366–7, Dan Patitucci; 368, sumikophoto/Adobe Stock; 369, NPS Photo; 371, Jose Luis Stephens/Alamy Stock Photo; 373, maxdigi/Adobe Stock; 375, Steve Cole Images/E+/Getty Images; 377, Jared Paisley; 379, steheap/Adobe Stock; 380–1, Hilary Yang; 383, Thomas Shahan; 385, jpldesigns/Adobe Stock; 386–7, Dan Fauss; 389, Charles Uniatowski Photography; 391, Abram Dickerson.

Since 1888, the National Geographic Society has funded more than 14,000 research, conservation, education, and storytelling projects around the world. National Geographic Partners distributes a portion of the funds it receives from your purchase to National Geographic Society to support programs including the conservation of animals and their habitats.

Get closer to National Geographic Explorers and photographers, and connect with our global community. Join us today at nationalgeographic.org/joinus

For rights or permissions inquiries, please contact National Geographic Books Subsidiary Rights: bookrights@natgeo.com

ISBN: 978-1-4262-2396-9

Printed in China

24/RRDH/1

The information in this book has been carefully checked and to the best of our knowledge is accurate. However, details are subject to change, and the publisher cannot be responsible for such changes, or for errors or omissions. Assessments of sites, hotels, and restaurants are based on the author's subjective opinions, which do not necessarily reflect the publisher's opinion.

HUNDREDS OF ADVENTURES TO EXPLORE

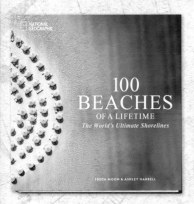
100 BEACHES OF A LIFETIME — The World's Ultimate Shorelines
FREDA MOON & ASHLEY HARRELL

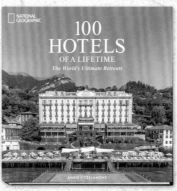
100 HOTELS OF A LIFETIME — The World's Ultimate Retreats
ANNIE FITZSIMMONS

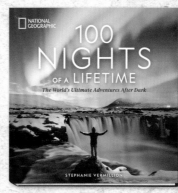
100 NIGHTS OF A LIFETIME — The World's Ultimate Adventures After Dark
STEPHANIE VERMILLION

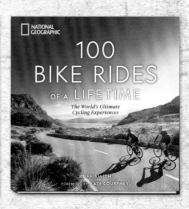
100 BIKE RIDES OF A LIFETIME — The World's Ultimate Cycling Experiences
ROFF SMITH FOREWORD BY KATE COURTNEY

100 DISNEY ADVENTURES OF A LIFETIME — Magical Experiences From Around the World
MARCY CARRIKER SMOTHERS FOREWORD BY JOE ROHDE

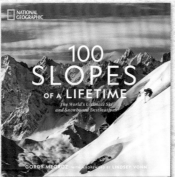
100 SLOPES OF A LIFETIME — The World's Ultimate Ski and Snowboard Destinations
GORDY MEGROZ WITH A FOREWORD BY LINDSEY VONN

100 DIVES OF A LIFETIME — The World's Ultimate Underwater Destinations

100 HIKES OF A LIFETIME — The World's Ultimate Scenic Trails